HOW TO HAVE
HAPPY CHILDREN

HOW TO HAVE HAPPY CHILDREN

THE LITTLE BOOK OF
TEN COMMANDMENTS
FOR PARENTS OF
TODDLERS TO TEENS

DR MARTIN J. COLES

RedDoor

Published by RedDoor
www.reddoorpublishing.com
© 2019 Martin J. Coles

The right of Martin J. Coles to be identified as author of this
Work has been asserted by him in accordance with sections
77 and 78 of the Copyright, Designs and Patents Act 1988

ISBN 978-1-910453-82-7

Poem on page v adapted from: 'This Be The Verse', *Collected
Poems* (2003) by Philip Larkin with permission of Faber and
Faber Ltd

Every effort has been made to trace copyright holders and to
obtain their permission for the use of copyright material. The
publisher apologises for any errors or omissions in the above list
and would be grateful if notified of any corrections that should be
incorporated in future reprints or editions of this book

A CIP catalogue record for this book is available from
the British Library

Cover design: ironicitalics.com
Typesetting: sheerdesignandtypesetting.com
Printed and bound in Denmark by Nørhaven

They need not mess you up, your mum and dad.
If they want you happy, which they do,
They will not give you faults they had
Nor add some extra, just for you.

If they were messed up in their turn
By fools in old-style hats and coats,
They don't now need to be soppy-stern
Nor half at one another's throats...

Adapted from 'This Be The Verse' by Philip Larkin

THE COMMANDMENTS

YOU SHALL NOT BE PERFECT

Parenthood is becoming rarer among the affluent populations of Western societies. Italy, Japan, Germany and Britain all have populations where the birth rate is levelling out and will probably soon decline. There are many theories about why this is happening: educated adults are choosing not to have children because they are prioritising their career, their leisure time and their personal adult relationships; potential parents are baulking at the cost of having children and the commensurate loss in their spending power that a child would entail; perhaps because many of today's young adults come from families affected by divorce or separation and were requisitioned as parent substitutes to their younger siblings or to their lonely parents, so that their parenting instincts were triggered at too early an age and now they have no motivation to start their own family; or are we, like other mammals put under stress, reacting to the overcrowding and uncertainty in our daily lives by not wanting to breed? You are different. You have taken an optimistic stance. If you are reading this you must believe in the future. You believe there will be a better tomorrow to live in. You have made this clear by having children. So now you want to make sure that your optimism is well-founded. Now that you have children, how do you make sure that you bring them up well? How can you help them to be happy?

Let's start the other way around. One way to help children be unhappy is to try to create them in your own image, to give in to the desire to try to create the child you would like to have, rather than helping your child to develop in their own good time to their fullest, in line with their natural endowment and their unique life history. Quite naturally parents control the family story while their children are young. The children are the subject of this story, the originators of its magic and appeal; but sometimes they remain simply, as it were, characters – individuals who have their being in the heads of their parents. A large part of the parental role is invested in keeping this story going, but it is perhaps unwise to treasure this story too much, to keep it too close to your heart, or to believe in it too much. It is important to realise the truth of the cliché that we don't own our children. Your children's futures are theirs to mould, not yours to control and oversee. Parenting is about gradually letting go, allowing your children to become the adults they want to be, not the ones you want them to be. Parenting is mostly about the now and not the tomorrow. Our job is to look after our children as well as we can for the present and to build their confidence and abilities so they can safely move away from the safe harbour of their childhood home and sail out into the world. Before then, children do have their own life, and sometimes what they need is different from what you think they need. If you only insist on your own story, instead of allowing the child to create a story of their own, then parenthood will become a litany of force, insistence and punishment. It will contain too much of the sound and voice of you, the parent. When you talk you can't listen. When you insist, you miss the opportunity to learn something new. Your child will be less than perfect, as you are. It is best to tolerate these imperfections and accept your child for who they are. Pushing a child to be someone they are not is a sure way to mess them up. The key to avoiding this is to concentrate on the process of parenting, and not on the outcome.

These ten commandments are intended to help you reflect on how to be the best you can be with your children, to help you to help them develop to the fullest. The ten commandments add up together to this one exhortation: make it your goal to raise children who are comfortable with who they are and pleased with the way they were brought up. There is a Chinese proverb, which translates approximately as, 'Nobody's family can hang out a sign saying "Nothing the matter here".' However, the happiest families are those in which each member acts with consideration and respect for the other family members. Happy children require you, as a parent, to think about the experiences you are having with your children, and they with you, reflecting on your behaviour and feelings and those of your child, and then deciding yourself on the best solutions to the formidable challenges of raising a child.

Raising children is often presented as if there were right or wrong answers to the many questions parents have about how to deal with their children. Actually it is more like a multiple choice test or perhaps a very long essay. No one who does not have an intimate knowledge of your child knows exactly what is right for him or her. One child responds well to positive reinforcement, while another can be managed only with a stern voice. One child is toilet trained at three but another, perhaps his sibling, at two. When my own children were small we were told to put our baby to bed on her front so that she would not choke if she was sick in the night. Later babies were put to sleep on their back or side because of research on sudden infant death syndrome. What to do? The answer is often that you know best. You do have an intimate knowledge of your child. We all have different realities. We all write our own book. Eventually you must learn to trust yourself.

I remember my own worries when my eldest daughter always hid behind my legs whenever she was introduced to new people, and refused to acknowledge them. I searched in child development books for an explanation. Neither of her parents was shy. Were we doing something wrong? Was there something wrong with her social development? Was something happening with her sibling that was causing this nervousness? Now grown-up, as an adult she has travelled extensively on her own, lived independently in France for a year and teaches undergraduates. There's nothing wrong with her social confidence.

Every part of raising children is chastening. Inevitable mistakes will be made, and one error is to imagine that you can be the perfect parent. You want to be the perfect parent of course, but this is simply not possible. Being a good parent is not a static accomplishment like learning to ride a bike or reading a book. It can only be a constantly developing capability. If you consider bringing up children is like writing a very long essay, then it's helpful to remember that the word essay derives from the French infinitive *essayer*, 'to try' or 'to attempt'. Being a parent is about trying to be the best you can be. So, relieve yourself of the burden of perfection.

In *The Tempest* Shakespeare paints a complicated relationship between Prospero and his daughter Miranda. When Prospero finds it possible to enlighten Miranda about her origins he says:

> *'Tis time*
> *I should inform thee further; lend thy hand*
> *And pluck my magic garment from me – so!*

The stage direction then states: 'Lays down his mantle.' Prospero, pointing to his robe, says, 'Lay there my art.' He had to stop being a magician and be content with being an ordinary father. No parent is a magician. Being a perfect parent can only be an ambition, an ambition in the face of an impossible task. In the moment, and for most people, being a good enough parent is difficult enough. Obviously we want to be role models because parental behaviour has a huge and significant influence on children, but it's tough to be perfect all the time, in fact it's impossible. Are you letting them down if they see you drinking into the early hours, if they see you losing your patience in a long queue at the ticket office, if they hear you ranting about the reckless driver who has just pulled out in front of your car without warning? If you worry about these things, then a moderate amount of guilt around your parenting is only a sign of your love and commitment to do the best you can to raise happy, well-balanced children. It is impossible to live the perfect life, but reassuring to know that being 'good enough' is enough. Better to focus on providing your children with a satisfying and interesting childhood than to spend time worrying about trying to bulletproof them for adulthood.

That phrase, a 'good enough' parent, comes from a famous book written over twenty-five years ago by the child psychotherapist Bruno Bettelheim when he was eighty-four years old. His title was in fact borrowed from the psychoanalyst and parenting expert Donald Winnicott, who first broadcast his idea of the 'good enough mother', the mother who wasn't perfect and was free to some extent to fail, on the BBC radio in the 1940s. The main theme of Bettelheim's book is that definitive answers and dogmatic theories of parenting should be rejected because no author can be aware of the total situation in a family and that 'how to' approaches imply that there is only one right way of doing things, and other approaches are wrong.

His advice is that any books about parenting should be about making suggestions to parents, to promote their ability to become 'good enough'. This short book, despite its title and the idea of 'commandments', takes Bettelheim's approach. *How to Have Happy Children* is not a preconceived equation for success with your children. The commandments may appear on the surface a set of rules, but they are in fact a recipe. As the old saying goes: 'Rules are for the obedience of fools and the guidance of wise men.' In a recipe you use your common sense and experience to add a little something more here, a little less of that ingredient there, a bit more of this and a little less of that. Following a recipe does not guarantee a good dish, but it is a guide that increases the chances of you getting things right. The 'commandments' are intended to make you feel secure in parenthood and less worried about what might possibly go wrong. Nobody can be perfect. Some things will inevitably turn out other than as you intended.

Like all parents you will make mistakes. Making mistakes and owning up to them is good modelling for children. If your child sees you are not perfect and you sometimes find things difficult, resolving those difficulties and talking about how you managed is good parenting. Trust your instincts. Learn from your mistakes. Have fun learning to be a good enough parent, and make the most of the moment. Your children will all too soon grow up. This fact becomes particularly clear when the moment of their childhood is gone, and you experience it only captured in photographs or videos. I have a particular picture of my daughters that I treasure. The two of them are sitting on a bench, wearing sun hats and looking out to sea. The photo is taken from behind and the eldest has her arm protectively around my younger daughter. I know I took the picture but I wish I could remember where we were, exactly how old they were when the photo was taken, what we talked about on that promenade, how they sounded and what they looked like when they slept that night. I wish I had not always been in such a hurry to get on to the next thing. I wish I had spent more time simply enjoying the moments like that time they sat together on the seaside bench.

Just as no parent can be perfect, no child can be perfect either, but every child has something they are naturally good at and love doing. Every child is special and it is important to appreciate what is special about your child. What it is that makes them unique? What is their spark? It may be their talents, their kindness or their optimistic personality. Their spark might be musical, athletic, intellectual or academic. Their spark will light their way. Look for some specific things you can help your child understand makes them special, rather than some vague 'You are so amazing'. It will give them a real sense of competence, direction and identity. And help your child realise that they have a special future ahead of them. It doesn't matter if your child's 'spark' doesn't lead to an obvious career. It doesn't matter if they do not become rich or famous. They don't need to be in the top team or get into a top university, but they have a unique personality, which they can use for the good of themselves and others, and you are looking forward to seeing it develop. This doesn't mean defining your child's character early on and sticking to that view. It is unwise to label your child extrovert or introvert, dominant or submissive, or to tell people that one of your children is the sporty one, the other the brainy one. As I learned when assuming at first that my eldest daughter was shy, you can't really know in what direction your child is heading until they are young adults. Just relax, allow your child to develop, and acknowledge and celebrate it when special aspects of their personality become obvious.

Even today I'm not sure what worked and what didn't with my children; what was my parenting and what was simply life. When my children were very small, I suppose I thought some day they would become who they were because of what I'd done. Now I know that isn't true. I was far from a perfect parent and I suspect that they simply grew into their true selves because they demanded in a thousand ways that I be there when they needed me, that I helped them when they required it, that I set down rules and boundaries when that was helpful to them, but otherwise that I let them be to grow themselves. That's what being a good enough parent means. You shall not be perfect! Mothers who set themselves impossible parenting standards and take on the lion's share of childcare themselves without support and become stressed as a result are doing their children no favours. A mother's stress has a negative impact on children. Let go of the pressure to be perfect and the pressure to be with your children all of the time. Take a collaborative approach to parenting. Children benefit when more than one person is involved and active in their lives, whether it be with your partner, grandparents, friends or nursery and day-care providers. Avoid the urge to micromanage your child's life. And in particular try to share the parenting burden between father and mother. Children involved with their father have higher self-esteem, better cognitive and social skills, fewer behavioural problems and higher academic achievement. You don't have to be perfect, just be engaged. So take note of the first commandment: You shall not be perfect.

YOU SHALL PREFER PRESENCE TO PRAISE

'If parents want to give their children a gift, the best thing they can do is to teach their children to love challenges, be intrigued by mistakes, enjoy effort, and keep on learning. That way their children don't have to be slaves of praise. They will have a lifelong way to build and repair their own confidence.' (Carol Dweck)

In his book *The Examined Life* the famous psychotherapist Stephen Grosz explains how he overhears his daughter's nursery assistant tell her one day, 'You've done the most beautiful drawing. Well done,' and on another day, 'Wow, you really are an artist.' Grosz found himself at a loss. He knew his daughter was not very good at drawing and he wondered how he could explain to the assistant why he would prefer it if she didn't praise his daughter.

That nursery assistant would wonder what the problem is. Nowadays we tend to lavish continuous praise on our children. I have been in a classroom in the USA where I timed how often students were told 'good job'. It was approximately every two minutes. The common belief is that praise breeds self-esteem and confidence, but recent research suggests that this simply isn't true. Praising a child as 'clever' may in fact be counterproductive and cause them to underperform and hold back effort and progress. If you are praised for doing something without advice about how to improve it, why not simply give up? If you've made the best drawing, why try to do better? And why would you try new things or experiment if your old way of doing things is given so much acclaim. 'If it ain't broke, don't fix it' is a motto children who are praised regularly will easily come to understand, and then they simply repeat the same performance and fail to progress.

In a famous study, looking at children aged ten and eleven, psychologists Carol Dweck and Claudia Mueller asked 128 children to solve a series of mathematical problems. The researchers gave each child just one sentence of praise after they had completed the first set of exercises. Some were praised for their intelligence, 'You did really well, you are so clever;' others were praised for their hard work, 'You did really well, you must have tried so hard.' Then the children were asked to try to solve a more difficult set of problems. The results were striking. Children who were praised for their effort displayed a greater willingness to solve the more challenging problems. They tried out new approaches and kept at it. If they started to struggle, they put it down to lack of effort, rather than poor intelligence, and they tried harder. The children who had been praised for being clever did less well. They chose mathematical problems that they knew they could complete, problems that confirmed what they already knew. When they started to struggle they showed less resilience than the other children and had a tendency not to stick at it. It seems that the brief joy created by being told that you are clever actually leads to a decrease in motivation and performance, and a corresponding drop in self-esteem and confidence. The researchers asked the children to write to students in another school telling them about their experience of the research exercise. Some of the 'clever' children lied, exaggerating how well they had done. Amazingly, all it had taken to make a dramatic difference in children's attitudes and performance had been one sentence of praise.

Perhaps the fact that we seem to be wedded to praising our children is a generational thing. In his book Stephen Grosz draws attention to Anne Enright's memoir *Making Babies*. Anne Enright talks about what she calls the old days in Ireland –

in fact the 1970s. She explains how mothers would automatically express disapproval of their children with exclamations such as 'She's a monkey' or 'She'll have me in an early grave'. Her point is that she grew up in a country where any kind of praise for a child was taboo. Of course this wasn't the case only in Ireland in the past. I tried with my own children to avoid what I saw at the time as the negative comments I regularly received from my own mother as a child. Whenever I did well or succeeded at something I was likely to hear her say: 'Look at you, Mr Big Head', or 'Don't you get too big for your boots now', or 'Who do you think you are – the cat's whiskers?'. I remember vividly when, at eleven years old, I passed the exam to go to one of the better schools near where we lived; the reaction from my parents couldn't have been cooler. 'Well done. Good lad. You're the best' were not phrases in their vocabulary. My parents believed sincerely in humility and I think, looking back now, they considered that praising their children was somehow a display of arrogance. 'Look at us, look what fantastic parents we are to bring up such wonderful, clever children.'

Saying one should be wary of offering too much praise is not of course to say you should be openly critical of your child. Thoughtless criticism is as harmful as empty praise, perhaps more so. In both cases you are not thinking carefully enough about your child and their world. Thoughtless praise, like thoughtless criticism, in effect expresses unconcern and lack of interest. Admiring your children and praising them regularly and saying how brilliant they are may raise your own self-esteem, but we now know that it won't do much for your child's sense of worth. So if praise doesn't build a child's self-esteem and confidence, what does? The answer is 'presence'.

Spend regular time with your children, ask them open-ended questions about themselves, about the world and how they see it, and actively listen to their responses. Not only will you learn all sorts of things that make your child unique, you'll also be demonstrating to them how to show care and concern for another person. I understand that recommending being present with your children goes against the grain of modern western lifestyles. Workers in the UK have traditionally had some of the longest working hours in Europe – working on average 42.7 hours a week. In parenthood surveys British parents often complain that they don't have enough time to spend with their children, saying, for instance, that they are often too tired at the end of a long working day and a tiring commute to read their child a bedtime story, even though that can potentially be one of the most satisfying times to spend with a child. Perhaps it is no coincidence that

British children often come near the bottom of lists that make a judgement about children's relative well-being in different countries. For instance in 2014, The Children's Society published a 'Good Childhood Report' which found that ten-to-twelve-year-olds in England ranked fourteenth out of the fifteen nations studied for happiness.

Although it might be difficult for some parents to hear, more family time, especially with older children, has been found to be essential to children's well-being. For instance, a long-term study by the University of Toronto and Bowling Green State University in Ohio found in 2015 that just six hours of dedicated family time each week, an average of fifty minutes a day, was linked to lower rates of delinquent behaviour in teenagers and better school performance. The study did not consider very young children, but with older children, mothers' working hours outside the home were not a significant matter, researchers said, but once children reached their teens, the amount of shared family time made a significant difference. Significantly though, the factor with the greatest impact on children's well-being was the stress level of their mother. Researchers said mothers who felt guilty at not spending enough time with their children could be making matters worse, because anxiety had a greater effect on their offspring than the amount of shared family time. In Sweden the government is testing six-hour days for employees who have families in some of its departments because it believes it will have a positive impact on family life and the well-being of their staff without actually affecting productivity.

One simple thing to do would be to sit down and eat with your children regularly. UK parents lag behind every single European country when it comes to eating the main meal of the day with their children. A survey of British households found that one in seven families never eat together at all due to the long hours culture and fragmented timetables. Yet eating together is much more than just sharing a meal, with a growing number of studies finding a direct link between the number of family meals and a child's emotional well-being. These studies include findings published in the *Journal of Adolescent Health* that show that family dinners give youngsters a feeling of belonging and security, and that children who have structured and social meal times have a more positive outlook, and higher sense of self-worth. They get better school marks and are less likely to start smoking or taking drugs in their teenage years. And the more that families eat together – breakfast, lunch or dinner – the greater the benefits.

Importantly, 'presence' is not just about being in the company of your children, perhaps reading the paper when they are playing with their toys, and certainly it doesn't mean continually talking to them so they have no space for their own play and reflection. It means thinking carefully about the place your child is in mentally and emotionally and taking your place alongside them there. I once worked with an education adviser named Jack Ouseby. Jack had a great way of simply being 'there' with children. He tells a story about visiting a group of six-year-olds who had recently been on a class visit to the zoo. He noticed particularly one boy deeply engaged in a drawing and sat down next to him, saying nothing. The boy was simply colouring in with an orange crayon between two wide parallel lines which ran from the top right-hand corner of the page, to the bottom left. After a while the boy turned and said, 'Hello, what's your name?'

'Jack,' said Jack, 'and what's yours?'

'Michael,' said the boy.

Nothing further was said for quite some while, but Jack continued to look carefully at the boy's picture. And then the boy turned to Jack and said, 'Tell you what, Jack; I'm bloody fed up with drawing this giraffe.'

Jack's quiet presence and intense concentration on the boy's crayoning had encouraged that young boy into an intimate comment he would never have used with his teacher. Jack would never praise a child for what they ought to be able to do. He would praise them if they did something really difficult. He would never praise a child who was simply playing or reading or drawing, but he would say 'Thank you' if they showed him a piece of their work, or explained something to him or had been especially kind to some other child. And he might comment on a child's effort in the kind of way that made the child think. 'That's an interesting picture of your mummy. I can only see two fingers on her hands. I wonder where the others have gone?' Jack's focus was always on what a child did, to try to understand it, and to react thoughtfully.

I once had the privilege of sitting next to a small girl on an aeroplane. Sadly, I think there are probably rules now, which mean that men on their own can't sit next to small girls on aeroplanes. I was reading a magazine and the small girl was reading a picture story and saying the words very quietly to herself. I listened for quite some while and then I said, 'Would you read to me. I'd like to hear that story.'

'Oh no,' she said, 'I can't read.'

'But I saw you,' I said. 'I saw you reading.'

'Well,' she said, 'I can read a little bit, but I don't usually tell anyone. Which page shall I read to you?'

Fathers in particular sometimes fall prey to the 'provider problem'. Often fathers show their love by working hard at their jobs in order to provide a good life for their children, but they are out of sight when they do this so their love for their children does not show through. Most children would much prefer to have fewer gifts and outings if it meant their father was present with them. Most children would prefer a dad who showed interest in talking to them and doing things with them, rather than simply buying them gifts. It is amazing how often men use work as an excuse for not spending time with their children, but it is possible to be creative about making time to be present with your children. Even if it is for only one day a week, leaving work early, and coming home to have dinner with the children (turning the television off during that time) will feel good to your children. As I pointed out above, the research clearly shows that families who eat together four nights a week or more reduce the risk of teenagers in particular getting into trouble by half.

One of the most fruitful ways of fathers being with their children is to go on 'dad dates'. If a father bothers to spend time alone with their children it generates an enormous feeling of well-being. The 'date' might only be to a fast food restaurant, or to a film, or to somewhere the child chooses, but it will be hugely worthwhile for the child if the father then listens and asks them about themselves, their friends, and what they are enjoying at school. Of course, it mustn't be an inquisition, and certainly not an opportunity to 'sort out' problems. Avoid being the plumber or the policeman. The plumber fixes things. The policeman makes judgements and arrests. 'Dad dates' are not the chance to fix things and certainly not to be judgemental or critical. They are the chance for light and friendly conversation, a chance to be together and send the message that you care and understand.

Being present as a parent builds a child's confidence because it lets them know they are worth thinking about. How can we ask a child to be attentive if we are not attentive to them? A child feeling that an adult is paying attention to them, is trying to think about them, is worth a lot more than meaningless praise, or even thoughtless presence. Observe. Listen. Prefer presence to praise.

YOU SHALL RESPECT CHANGE

It is sometimes difficult not to envy our children their riches – their growing physical strength and intelligence, their liveliness, joy and wonder at the world. Everybody can only once for the first time see the sea, or for the first time feel floating flakes of snow on their face, or for the first time fly in an aeroplane. There cannot be many parents who have not, at some point, wished to reverse places with their children so that they could recapture that wonder. And many parents will wish they could reverse places simply so that they might have an even longer future stretching out ahead of them. You don't have to be a parent to feel envious of someone who is in most respects your junior. A teacher can envy their student, a football coach their player. There will always be people younger than us who are cleverer, more attractive, better off financially. But it is not helpful for a parent to get caught up in this kind of thinking, for at the extreme it will cost a parent their peace of mind and threaten the loss of their relationship with their child. A psychotherapist might point out that when we envy our children we deceive ourselves. We are thinking too little of them and too much of ourselves. Parents who want happy children have to find a way to unhook themselves from the net of wishing they were younger, to accept themselves and their place in time. Only then will you succeed with your children and enjoy your child's growing physical strength and intelligence, their liveliness, joy and wonder at the world. There is an African proverb that says: 'If you want to walk quickly, walk alone – but if you want to walk far, walk together.' Your children are following your footsteps. You can be proud of them and take pleasure in their successes.

One way to escape the net of envy and to be close to your children is to change with them. Of course managing change is notoriously difficult for many human beings, a fact reflected in this old joke: 'How many professors does it take to change a light bulb? … Answer: Change? Don't let that be said of staff at this university!' But more seriously, change can be so difficult in fact that even in the face of extreme physical danger, some people simply cannot change. There are horrific stories of office workers in the south tower of the World Trade Center carrying on with their normal working routines even after they knew that a plane had hit the north tower in 2001. And television footage of the fire that killed fifty-six people at the football stadium in Bradford in 1985 shows fans continuing to watch the game without a thought about moving towards the exits, even though they can see the flames.

We tend to resist change. Committing ourselves to even a small change is sometimes more frightening than carrying on as before. You can check out this feeling in a small way yourself, by placing your wristwatch on the other wrist to that you normally use. This little bit of discomfort moves you out of your comfort zone to something you are not used to. Sometimes you will look at your empty wrist; you will still look to the past. Ah, look how soon you put your watch back on the wrist you are used to – the sigh of a comfortable habit. If this tiny change is so uncomfortable, is it any wonder that bigger changes disorient us? This feeling is normal and understandable. We want to know what new story we are stepping into before we exit the old one.

There is a lot of evidence that shows that change isn't easy. I once talked to a medic who told me: 'If you look at people after a serious heart operation, two years later ninety per cent of them have not changed their lifestyle. Even though they have a very bad disease and they know they should change, for whatever reason they can't. Many still carry on with their unhealthy lifestyles.' Serious heart disease is among the most serious of personal health crises and it doesn't motivate people to change even when they are given accurate information about their situations. These people know their very life is in jeopardy and still they don't change. It's the same when people with lung cancer don't give up smoking.

I know that change is not easy myself. I used to try to keep fit by attending a gym two or three times a week, but slowly I stopped finding time to go and I let my membership lapse. And then I didn't do any exercise, and I quite liked being able to ignore that nagging voice, which told me I had to get down to the gym. For two years I did no exercise. Now the normal assumption is that when we fail to change our ways it's because we lack discipline, we are simply too lazy to change and too lacking in ambition to do things differently. In fact there is a body of research which suggests not that we are lazy or insincere, but that we have become immune to change. The language is really important here. An immune system is benign. It protects us. In other words the reason we don't change is because we are unconsciously protecting ourselves from what we *think* will be the consequences of the change. In my case it was the hard work of getting down to the gym and using up time I wanted to use to do other things. So we have to develop a different immune system. I did that by stopping thinking about the gym and hired a rowing machine for my home office. I thought this would be easy. I don't have to drive anywhere; there it is staring at me. I only have to sit down and start rowing each day. Actually it sat there for two or three weeks before I took the first step. That first step to change was the hardest, but it became easier to get on to it the second time. Now, to be honest, I miss it if I haven't done some exercise for a day or two. I have changed my immune system. My body regularly reminds me that I need to exercise. In the same way, when it comes to making changes in what we do, we need to find ways to change the immune system that is stopping us from making the right changes. You can apply this thinking to all sorts of things – from the need to take the dog for a walk when you've got low energy levels to much more important changes that you need to make when you are bringing up children.

Change always involves loss, loss of the old way of doing things. And as children grow this is often a melancholy loss. Oh, how we wish we could still play aeroplanes at mealtimes, flying that spoon into baby's mouth to hear her giggle. How we wish we could still kick that football around in the garden and score goals against our son the goalie. Now, of course, he is helping to cook the meals and she is off playing with her friends. Inconveniently, the world refuses to stand still. Bark scraping gives way to slate, which gives way to quills, and then to ink pens, and then keyboards and then voice recognition software…but some values never change. We know that happy and successful adults usually need integrity, self-confidence, self-discipline, self-reliance and resilience, and that's not going to change. So what are the crucial areas of experience that my child is having that are different to those I had when I was a child, but are simply part of the changing world I should accept? And which are the areas of experience that reflect the fundamental values that I believe will allow my child to grow up to be a kind, considerate and happy adult? If your child's experience compromises these values, then it is entirely right that you change those experiences rather than your attitude towards them.

A long time ago, when my children were young, I was sitting in the lounge watching television, having put the children to bed an hour or so ago. Suddenly I heard a loud bump on the ceiling. What in the world had happened? I ran into the children's bedroom to see my seven-year-old daughter huddled up in her duvet on the floor. She had fallen out of bed, a quite dangerous accident since her bed was on the top level of a set of bunk beds. So I asked her, 'What happened, sweetheart? Are you OK? Did you have a bad dream?'

'No.'

'Did you get caught up in the duvet? Did you slide under the safety bar?'

'No,' she said sleepily, 'I'm all right. I'm fine.'

So I tucked her up, kissed her on the cheek and started to leave the room, and just as I was about to go out of the door, a small voice behind me said, 'Dad, I stayed too near where I got in.'

Have you stayed too near where you got in with your children? I plead guilty to this fault. Sometimes I stayed too near where I got in with my children. For a long time I held on to the belief that they should spend time reading books, as my generation did as children, rather than viewing a screen, be that a TV or computer screen – until I realised that this was not a reasonable position. Their world was a screen world as well as a book world and I simply had to accept that. On the other hand, when writing letters of thanks became a chore for them, and 'thank you letters' fell out of fashion, I still considered that they ought to express gratitude for gifts – this was an important habit for them to acquire – either with a phone call, or an email or text.

Bringing up children is a journey, and an adventure. Adventure inevitably has within it a state of mind that includes feelings of uncertainty about the journey, perhaps a bit of fear. In fact if it didn't have this element it would hardly be a challenge and thus an adventure. Of course, fear extended to terror is not an adventure, but normally as the journey progresses feelings of satisfaction and enjoyment overtake the fear. To make progress on any adventure – to keep up with the moving forwards – we need to have initiative and flexibility. Similarly in our relationship with our children, a view of our journey with them should not be constrained by history, but shaped by a view that new things can be done, and the challenge is to work out how. You are not going to be a great parent because of your lovely house, or the number of holidays you take your children on. No one is going to admire you as a parent because your children have passed all their school exams. They are going to admire you if your children are happy. That is only going to happen if you move forwards with them. It's been said that if an Englishman gets promoted from the inferno of hell to paradise he will still gather a group around him and talk about the good old days. The British are famous for looking to the past, and sometimes that is easier because looking to the future can be awkward and discomforting. But the world has changed from the one you were in as a child. Do you want your child prepared for their future or your past?

Having said all this it is sometimes important to look back to acknowledge what you have achieved in bringing up your children. Anyone who has been on a sailing boat will know that when you are moving forwards and looking to where you are heading it is sometimes difficult to judge the speed until you look behind you to see how much wash you are making. The same is true of being a parent. So if you look behind at the last few years what would you see? Well, far too much development and change in your child to list them all I would think. Children's development is never stagnant and very rarely do their changes happen in a big bang. More often changes are imperceptible, everyday small miracles that happen when you are not looking, but when you look back, then you can see them as significant. Every time a small child learns to tie a knot, or starts to read, or an older child discovers the pleasure in giving a gift, or finds a passion for a subject or activity that will eventually determine their career, these are the real moments of change and development. The obvious cliché is that saying: 'The only constant is change'. It is a cliché that cannot be but true with children. If your children are to be happy they need parents who are comfortable with that fact. After all, the future is not just some place your child is going, but one you are creating together. The paths to that future are sometimes randomly found but often also can be made. Respect change!

YOU SHALL NOT MAKE FOR YOURSELF A FALSE IDOL IN SCREEN TIME, BUT COVET SLEEP TIME

Young people in the UK are among the world's most enthusiastic users of digital technology. Ofcom's 2017 survey found that children aged five to fifteen spend on average more than two hours a day online. And they use their own kit. Twenty-one per cent of children aged three to four have their own tablet or games console and eighty-three per cent of children aged twelve to fifteen own a smartphone. Mothers and fathers of the digital age are well aware of the growing competition for their children's attention, and they're bombarded at each turn of the page or click of the mouse with both cutting-edge ideas and new-found worries about technology's effect on their children. Computer technology has ushered in a new era of mass media, bringing with it both significant benefits and substantial concerns about the effect on children's well-being. Although we tend to see these issues as being new, similar promises and concerns have accompanied each new wave of media technology throughout the past century: films in the early 1990s, radio in the 1920s and television in the 1940s. With the introduction of each of these technologies proponents touted the benefits for children, while opponents voiced fears about exposure to inappropriate commercial pressures, and to sexual and violent content.

Initial research concerning each innovation has tended to focus on issues of access and the amount of time children are spending with the new medium. As use of the technology became more prevalent research shifted to issues about content and its effects on children. Thinking about children's use of computers is again following this pattern. But the increased level of interactivity – with games and social media platforms – and with the communication features of the internet, there is heightened promise of greatly enriched learning matched by significant concerns related to the increased risk of harm. Some argue that new technology benefits children by opening up new worlds to them while others say that new media might be used as a substitute for real life, undermining children's moral development and negatively affecting their physical development. In the face of these debates, which swirl among parents and in the press and public policy forums, what is a parent to think and what approach might they take? When every school appears to have different policies on use of technology how can a parent know what they should let their child do online and how old should they be when you let them do it? Society does after all rely on parents as the primary gatekeepers for safeguarding children from the media's potentially harmful effects. For instance, no expert will give you the right age for a child to start using a smartphone or social media even if it seems clear that most wouldn't recommend giving a smartphone to a primary age child. The American Academy of Pediatrics offers gold standard advice, which includes not letting under twos view screens at all. In fact, in April 2017 Bill and Melinda Gates admitted that their children had not been allowed smartphones until they were fourteen years old. Academic researchers insist that there is still no evidence that mere screen time causes harm, but the question is about opportunity cost. What are children missing out on when they spend most of their time on their screens? If children aged three to four are spending eight hours a week online, as Ofcom suggests, what offline skills are they not learning? Who are they not talking to? What fine motor skills are they not developing? What real world problem-solving skills are they failing to develop? What emotional experiences are they missing out on?

One problem is that for the most part children are adapting themselves to the adult world when they are online. How can that be right? If a child of five likes his plastic truck we are hardly likely to buy him a heavy goods vehicle. If a child of fourteen says he wants to drive we are unlikely to say 'OK' then; but nearly one child in ten now has an iPhone at five years of age. Getting a smartphone for transfer to secondary school is the new norm because at this age, a BBC survey in 2016 found, almost four out of five of them have a social media account. Many parents sign up on their children's behalf. It is not surprising that a lot of parents are confused about whether or not technology is messing up their children. While experts slug it out parents find it increasingly hard to know what to do, except perhaps to do what many experts advise, which is to approach tablets and smartphones in the same way you would a first car for your child. Only give it at the age you think your child can handle it properly. And let them know that even then they won't be driving alone – you'll be sitting in the passenger seat and watching their driving.

It is now commonplace to say that the world is changing fast and the pace of that change is accelerating. Google processes over one billion web searches each day. The number of text messages sent each day overtook the number of people on the planet back in 2007. In the decade I was born into, the 1950s, one computer filled a large room. Today immeasurably more computing power can be held in your hand than was used to put a man on the moon. Young children can access more information in a week than their grandparents might access in a lifetime. Our children have hardly known a moment when the entire world was not available in the palm of their hand. Now they don't have to ask parents for answers. Whereas once in the past they might have asked Mummy, 'Why is the sea blue?', now they simply ask Siri or Alexa. Even twenty years ago surveys were discovering that children between two and five were using computers for an average of half an hour per day, and were expressing content preferences almost as soon as they were exposed to this medium, so imagine what a survey taken today might find.

It is not surprising then that as young people spend more time with their gadgets – phones, tablets, laptops, smart TVs, fitbits, smart watches, games consoles – there are many voices calling for a cull of digital machines for young children or at least a digital detox. However, the fear that technology socially isolates and intellectually damages children has no real basis in evidence and in fact a number of studies show positive impact both on social skills and intellectual development; but the parent's role is critical in supporting children in their use of technology to ensure that the potential benefits are achieved.

I chose not to succumb to fear of the new or accept over-simplistic generalisations about the harm technology can cause. When it comes to technology resistance is futile but knowledge is power. On the one hand try not to be naïve about the effect devices might have on your child, but on the other to dismiss this new world as totally toxic would be a mistake. Best to get up to speed yourself and encourage your child to use tech in the smartest way possible. Nobody believes that setting hard limits is the right approach, but many do suggest that you monitor screen time in the same way you monitor how many hours' sleep your child gets or how much sugary food they are eating. There is nothing inherently evil about an iPad or online games. Electronic devices can be a very powerful educational resource if used correctly. It only becomes problematic if a child's life entirely revolves around technology. It is important not to forget that playing board games, climbing trees and playing I-spy on long car journeys may seem old-fashioned occupations but such leisure pursuits carry benefits that are as important as those derived from using Wikipedia; that taking part in adult conversations at meal tables continues to have many benefits; and that real time interaction with friends is often more valuable than spending time on social media sites. Of course, with young children computers and other electronic devices should supplement not replace highly valuable early childhood toys, activities and materials, such as paints, crayons, building blocks, writing materials, sand and water, and imaginative play equipment. If you feel your child is spending too long looking at a screen and not the real world, simply take the device out of their hands. You are the parent – it is important to remember that you have control. If your child uses electronic devices all day long, then don't let them take a device to bed. Read together in the bedroom instead, or play drawing games.

On the other hand, we have a duty to prepare children for their future, not our past. They have to learn to use social media and the internet responsibly, so it is not helpful to ban them altogether. Rather, limit access by time and also by subject. Allow your children to go there for specific things rather than randomly, and don't allow them to spend hours looking at YouTube clips of cute fluffy cats, or much worse. Take an interest in your children's interests.

If they get lost in a digital world, then you need to rescue them.

So we need to keep under examination the culture and attitudes to technology in our homes – to remain receptive, open-minded and critically aware of developments in technology in order to understand what impact they might have on our children. A certain scepticism about the use of technology is actually quite healthy. The idea that an app on an iPad can teach our children maths better than a teacher can is open to question. As is the idea that a small child can learn all they need by sitting in front of a screen rather than being out exploring the real world. On the other hand, nobody presumably wants their child to grow up beautifully equipped for a world that no longer exists. We need to engage, motivate and prepare our children for a new world. For most of our children information technology is no more intimidating than the TV or toaster is for us. Of course, if you are intimidated by a toaster then there is no hope for you! A Hebrew proverb makes this point in another way: 'Do not confine your children to your own learning, for they have been born in another time.'

If the distraction of technology continues to be a challenge and concern to parents, one answer to our ambivalence may well be to recognise and accept it.

That perspective allows us to see that like other ages before this one, all is not promise and all is not peril. Technology is neutral, neither good nor bad, except as it is used for good or ill. A bishop responded to a statement that man might fly one day with, 'Sir, you blaspheme. Flight is for angels.' The speaker was Bishop Milton Wright, father of Orville and Wilbur Wright, inventors of one of the earliest flying machines. The answer to the inevitability of your children having technology at their fingertips is control and direction.

Increasingly savvy mothers and fathers are harnessing technology to help them become the parents they aspire to be. Thanks to increasingly sophisticated apps and websites, technology can become less of an intrusion into family life and more of an enabler into creating a better family life. For new parents technology offers shortcuts to mundane tasks. Just as a washing machine liberated women from washdays each week in the past, so apps can take over some of the more mundane organisational work of being a parent, such as scheduling and record keeping, allowing mums and dads to engage and be more present with their children, to give them that clichéd but all important 'quality time'. An app called Baby Bundle, for instance, offers smart tools and trackers for pregnancy and child development.

Another app called Shae remotely monitors blood sugar levels of children with type 1 diabetes, via a sensor implanted painlessly in the child's arm, and sends the information to the parent's iPhone. That means the child can go out to play unaccompanied. The advice contained in many of these apps is a godsend for parents who are midnight worriers. And helpfully too some apps quickly connect parents to communities of other parents offering peer support, thereby assuaging one of the worst side effects of early parenthood – isolation. So it's wrong to demonise technology. It is here to stay and can be a force for good if used properly.

And once again remember, if your children are tuning you out at the touch of a button, then you should take charge of your child's use of technology. If you think they are too wedded to a machine, take the machine off them, or turn it off. Having an iPhone is not a fundamental human right, and shutting it down is not child abuse, however much your child might think of it as their entitlement. Do not have a crisis of authority. And if this approach worries you at all then perhaps read *The Collapse of Parenting: How We Hurt Our Kids When We Treat Them Like Grown-Ups* by Leonard Sax. There is also another expert that I would recommend on this subject. Noël Janis-Norton calls for parents to take charge and reclaim phones and tablets, using screen time as a reward to be earned.She suggests that if children have to earn their screen time then they are more likely to respect their devices, and respect you! She also suggests that if you restrict screen time, for teenagers in particular, they smile more, engage in more interesting conversations, are generally in a better mood, and find it easier to get up in the mornings. Perhaps institute a drop zone in the hallway of your house where machines are held until the right to use them has been earned, e.g. so many points for finishing homework or for going to bed on time.

In the home, placement of the device plays a determining role in how it is used. Early studies suggested that in the past more than half of families placed computers in children's bedrooms rather than in a more common family area, which might indicate that parents did not monitor their children's use and that computer use might be isolating. Now, however, with tablets and phones often taking over to a large extent from the old PC and with email and chat rooms in common use, this picture has changed somewhat. Computer use is a source of conversation and interaction among many family members today. There is a kind of Jekyll and Hyde phenomenon: your children need the internet and there are many benefits to be derived from it, but if they do go online without you, it can be worrying. Monitoring, using filters, and looking for safe and appropriate websites are all personal and private solutions by which parents can try to assure themselves that there is no need to be terrified of their children's use of the internet. Many non-profit groups provide websites of parent resources with tips on how to use the internet safely and productively, for instance:

https://www.nspcc.org.uk/preventing-abuse/keeping-children-safe/online-safety/

http://www.saferinternet.org.uk

So are you engaged in the exhausting struggle to separate your child from their iPhone or tablet computer? Over the past ten years screen time has crept up relentlessly. According to figures from the tech industry's advice body, Internet Matters, children between eleven and sixteen post online on average twenty-six times a day. Even when adults impose daily limits on screen time children admit to ignoring them. Perhaps it is time to rethink the way we view smartphones. First of all they are not phones. They are high-powered computers, far more powerful than even laptops were ten years ago. One of the key limits parents should impose is digital sunset, i.e. devices are removed between one and two hours before bedtime. Bedrooms should be sensory deprivation zones so that children can quieten themselves ready for sleep and not be excited by entertainment centres. The old-fashioned bedtime story had that good purpose of course and it is no less relevant today. There is a clear link between using devices late at night and sleep deprivation. But although a total ban might seem the only solution, it does not have to be an all or nothing approach. One phone-free day per week is a good start and 'no phones at meal times' another reasonable rule. Children may complain that they will lose their social lives but it is simply not true. They have friends for lots of reasons and accessibility to social media is just one factor. It is important not to worry about upsetting your children. There are lots of things that parents have to do because it is the right thing to do in your child's best interests, even though the child may not understand. Even better is for children to recognise themselves the symptoms of smartphone overuse, whether it's eye strain or irritability. Parents have got to say: 'It's not that I don't want you to use social networks or online games but your social life and games playing should also be happening in the real world.' Some children will welcome a reason not to feel pressured to respond to constant notifications. It's better to offer screen-free days as rewards rather than punishments and an opportunity to connect as a family and spend time together.

One problem with enforcing screen rules on children is that we adults are on our devices too much ourselves. If you keep a digital diary for a week you may well find that you are using a screen as much as your children. So weekends are a good time for the whole family to have a screen-free day. Children will have no problem with this if it is a rule for the whole family. Or consider Time Tokens (timetokens.com), a scheme whereby children can 'buy' screen time from their parents using vouchers. Point out to your child that overuse of social media can actually restrict the ability to build friendships. So encourage them to join clubs, classes and teams where they can make real friendships, valuing face-to-face interactions over 'likes' and 'followers'. Children who will thrive in adulthood are those who are open and adaptable with the ability to collaborate. It's very difficult to learn this online. It isn't reasonable to think that you can ban screens entirely, and if you did you would certainly not be preparing your child for their future world. But restricting uses in these ways protects them from the social pressures that accompany screen time.

Children's mental health must also be a consideration. Parents need to protect their children from the worst elements of digitalised childhood.

Children can plug themselves into devices which give them autonomy and independence, but as a parent you have a responsibility to safeguard them in those environments. The most important thing you can do in this regard is to give your children skills to cope when things go wrong. Even if your child has no interest in becoming a software engineer, being comfortable with screen technology will help them in a world where technology is a fundamental part of life. Coding is now part of the national curriculum and there are apps and games that show children that coding can be creative and fun. There is also an organisation that runs after-school clubs for nine to eleven year olds (codeclub.org).

One of the main dangers to a child's mental health is lack of sleep. Device use becomes particularly problematic if screen time is taken late at night and interferes with young children's sleep. Late night gadget use has been implicated in sleep deprivation in a number of studies. Researchers in China surveyed a cross-section of children aged nine to thirteen to find out about their sleep quality. More than 6000 children took part in the survey, which asked about sleep habits, homework, commute to school, how much time they spent on after-school activities and using electronic devices. Girls were likely to sleep less than boys and to go to bed later, a gender split that became wider as children got older. But the most important finding was that after-school activity, and in particular homework and mobile device tasks, were keeping children awake later. Late bedtime and less sleep were associated with more time using electronic devices after school. This is a problem. Significant sleep deprivation, especially among teenagers, is potentially damaging to mental health. Children who have too little sleep can become prone to negative emotions such as anger and depression. Although it may take determination, parents who care for their child's well-being must take a firm line with this problem. This means creating no-go areas in the house for technology, especially bedrooms, and no-go times, such as family meal times and the period leading up to bedtime. Janis-Norton points out that the blue light emitted by electronic screens suppresses the production of melatonin, a chemical that is released into the blood stream to make us feel sleepy. So over-use of screens just before bedtime means children who are tired and are more likely to be irritable. She also says that tired children will have decreased motivation and concentration and a tendency to over-sensitivity. The *Journal of Sleep Research* has numerous academic articles demonstrating the negative effects of too little sleep. And limiting screen time in favour of sleep seems also to have positive benefits. Research published in *The Lancet Child & Adolescent Health* journal has found that limiting children's recreational screen time (i.e. out of school use) to under two hours per day, and having sufficient sleep and physical activity is linked to improved cognition, the mental process of acquiring knowledge and understanding. Researchers in this study discovered, by analysing American children's data for eight to eleven year olds, that the more closely children stuck to their recommendation of less than two hours' recreational screen time and a good night's sleep the better their cognition.

What is a good night's sleep for children of different ages?

The National Sleep Foundation (www.sleepfoundation. org) issues guidelines:

- For toddlers (1–2 years) 11–14 hours

- For pre-schoolers (3–5 years) 10–13 hours

- For school age children (6–13 years) 9–11 hours

- For teenagers (14–17 years) 8–10 hours

The NHS has very similar guidelines suggesting that children who do not nap during the day need eleven hours' sleep at age five and ten hours at age nine. A minimum of eight to nine hours' sleep on school nights is also recommended for teenagers by the NHS. So, be strict about bedtime. Sleep has proven advantages for memory and performance. Sleep deprivation, on the other hand, makes children, just like adults, more prone to depression. It's not widely understood that the average teenager, for instance, needs eight or nine hours' sleep a night to be able to cope with the day ahead and their own physical and neurological growth.

If your child refuses to go to bed when you tell them then you can develop practices that can help – no screens in the bedroom and a routine every night, something calm and not related to schooling. And if we also turn our own lights out at a reasonable hour and get a good night's sleep that will only make parenting easier. If bedtime is a battle, build routines and set an appropriate bedtime for the age of your child, then stick to it consistently. While there are rough guidelines of between nine and eleven hours for six to thirteen year olds, most parents will know how much sleep their children really need in order to wake well and cope with the next day, but messing with routine can have the same effect as jet lag, affecting the body's circadian rhythms. If they are old enough you can sit down with your child and work out an after-school routine of activities and bedtimes and then display it somewhere so everyone knows it is an agreement.

A Canadian study conducted by Public Health Ontario in 2017 found that if parents don't impose consistent limits youngsters are 71 per cent less likely to get the sleep they need. Those with set bedtimes, on the other hand, are 59 per cent more likely to get the sleep they need. If children are not well rested it can have a detrimental impact on the whole of family life. Children who do not get enough sleep are more likely to be more badly behaved, moodier and have trouble concentrating – the same effects that lack of sleep has on adults! Furthermore, the lack of time in the evening for parents to be together without children has been found to have a detrimental effect on the parents' relationship because parents don't get time to talk to each other and because of the rising stress levels with children not going to bed.

If left to just one parent to enforce bedtime it's going to be difficult. A united front is best so children know that you mean business and don't try to play one parent off against the other – often the parent who arrives home later and wants to spend time with the children before they are put to bed.

Even if it is for only twenty minutes at the end of the day your child should do something to wind down – something that is not screen related. Teach your child to be kind to themselves and to create space to think and unwind. Give children a warning of time left before bedtime and then be firm. And tell them of how you will respond to any requests after they are in bed, i.e. they will be dealt with in the morning. Often younger children try to drag out the process by saying they are hungry or thirsty or are missing their favourite toy, so make sure those things are dealt with before they are finally in bed. With older children many experts recommend removing phones at a certain time at night, say nine o'clock, at least an hour before they are expected to go to sleep. 'To make it more likely that children will be tired by bedtime, all screens should be switched off a couple of hours beforehand,' says Janis-Norton. You have to accept unpopularity to set clear boundaries. There are no rule books though for the specific personality of your child. You just have to use your instincts, embrace the world your children live in, but help them navigate through it.

So, finally, here are a few practical things you can do to ensure that you do not make for yourself a false idol in screen time, but covet sleep time. All of them ask you, as a parent, to put yourself in control.

- Encourage your child to talk to you about how they use the internet and show you what they do. Discuss with them the kinds of things they might come across. A good time to talk is when they get a new device or mention a new website.

- Encourage your child to use their tech devices in a communal area, such as the living room or kitchen, and set up a user account for your child. If you think they aren't old enough to have a mobile phone or tablet, stay firm and explain the reasons why.

- Activate parental controls on your home broadband, all devices, including mobile phones, and games consoles. Safe search settings can also be activated on Google (and other search engines), YouTube and on entertainment sites like iTunes, iPlayer and Netflix.

- Be aware that if your child is accessing the internet using public Wi-Fi they may not have safety features active. Some providers are part of family friendly Wi-Fi schemes with filters to block inappropriate content. Look out for friendly Wi-Fi symbols, such as Mumsnet Family Friendly Wi-Fi, when you're out and about.

- Agree and set boundaries with your child or have a family agreement for their internet use, including when and where they can use portable devices and for how long.

- Start discussions about social networking early. Talk to children about the benefits and risks of social networking before they join any sites.

- If your child does have a social networking profile, teach them to block or ignore people and how to set strict privacy settings. Request that you or someone you both trust becomes their 'friend' or 'follower' to check that conversations and posts are appropriate.

- Check the age ratings that come with games, apps, films and social networks. They are a good guide to whether they're suitable for your child. For example, the age limit is thirteen for several social networking sites, including Facebook and Instagram.

- Be clear what your child can and can't do online – where they can use the internet, how much time they can spend online, the sites they can visit and the type of information they can share. Agree with your child when they can have a mobile phone or tablet.

- The best way to find out what your child is doing online is to ask them to tell you about what they do and what sites they like to visit. If they are happy to, ask them to show you. Talk to them about being a good friend online.

- Use airplane mode on your devices when your child is using them so they can't make any unapproved purchases or interact with anyone online without your knowledge.

- It's a good idea to talk to any older children about what they're doing online and what they show to younger children. Encourage them to be responsible and help keep their younger siblings safe.

- Use safe search engines, such as Swiggle or KidzSearch. You can save time by adding these to your 'favourites'. Safe search settings can also be activated on Google and other search engines.

- Talk to your child about what the internet is and explore it together so you can show them all the great fun and educational things they can do.

- Keep your devices out of reach and set passwords on all your internet-enabled devices and don't share them. Then you'll know when and where your child is accessing the internet. You can also make sure they're not making additional purchases when they're playing games or using apps.

- Set your homepage to a child-friendly site, such as CBeebies, and create a user account for your child on the family computer or device, which only allows access to sites you've chosen.

- You can choose safe, fun and educational online games to play with your child that you'll be confident about them exploring. You can find good free of charge examples from companies such as Disney Junior and Fisher-Price.

- It's never too early to start setting boundaries. Set some rules about how long your child can spend online and how long before bedtime devices have to be switched off.

- Keep talking and stay interested in what they're doing. Don't be afraid to bring up challenging issues with older children, such as sexting, pornography and cyberbullying. It could be embarrassing, but you'll both benefit from the subjects being out in the open.

- Your child can set privacy settings on most social networking sites so that only close friends can search for them, tag them in a photograph or share what they've posted.

- Talk to your teenager about being responsible when they're online. Children often feel they can say things online that they wouldn't say face-to-face. Teach them to always have respect for themselves and others online.

- Let them know that anything they upload, email or message could stay around forever online. Remind them they should only do things online that they wouldn't mind you, their teacher or a future employer seeing. Get them to think about creating a positive digital footprint.

- Remind them how important it is not to give in to peer pressure to send inappropriate comments or images. Point them to apps, such as Zipit, which will help them deal with these types of requests.

- One test for when a child is ready is to ask them what they intend to do with the technology they are asking for – they should be able to say what they want it for and to recognise which bits of it are useful to them.

YOU SHALL TAKE CARE OF YOUR CHILD'S FRIENDSHIPS

It used to be thought that children were naturally self-centred, inconsiderate and often cruel to each other, but more recent research has found that children are in fact overwhelmingly cooperative even when observation by adults is extremely discreet, and friendship building can start at a very early age. A Children's Society study found that forty per cent of two years olds report having a favourite playmate, and by four years old this has risen to sixty per cent.

Of course every parent wants their child to enjoy friendships. Learning to make close, lasting and genuine relationships is part of growing up. Any parent will enjoy watching their child's friendships with other children flourish and seeing how their friendships build their confidence and social skills. For adults having friends provides emotional support and promotes a feeling of well-being. Children's friendships are no different in this respect, but are also very important for their social and emotional development. Through friendships children learn how to relate to others and they develop social skills as they teach each other how to be good friends. As parents and adults we might look back to remember how making friends as children helped us to develop a sense of self-worth, educated us in dealing with conflict and disagreements, and enabled us to learn how to interact with our peers and colleagues day-to-day. Your present friendships probably also offer a valuable source of support, love, protection and influence outside the family. These aspects of friendship are similarly important in children's growth. Children who have friends are more likely to be self-confident and perform better academically at school than those without friends or at least with few friends. Socially, children develop more quickly if they have friends they can talk to at school; lessons and free time are more fun and productive if a child has friends. On the other hand, when children have difficulty in making friends or in keeping them, it often leads to them feeling lonely and unhappy with themselves.

What modern psychology tells us about friendships that go wrong is that children reflect the influence of the culture around them. They will imitate destructive as well as cooperative tendencies that they see around them – a fact that has obvious implications for how parents relate to one another. This phenomenon is evident in The Children's Society study, which found that of the fifteen countries surveyed, UK children had some of the most fraught social relationships – British children were more likely than children elsewhere to say that they had been left out from a friendship group at least once in the past month. One reason the report suggests for this was that we are among the biggest consumers of reality TV and competition-based programmes in the world, where relationships can be malicious and judgemental. Children were imitating the style of relationships they saw displayed in these programmes.

However, most children will make a serious effort to make and keep friends. When The Children's Society asked young people what made their childhood happy, friendship was a factor they mentioned most often. For a child, having friends who they can be themselves with is an important factor in making them feel good about themselves. It builds self-esteem because they know that friendship is a choice – whereas they didn't choose you! So how, as a parent, can you help your child develop meaningful and lasting friendships?

Well, first, it is well to remember that lasting friendships are quite difficult to maintain for children. My youngest daughter had a special girlfriend during her time in primary school. They left school each day arm in arm and gave each other a hug before saying goodbye, until tomorrow. This friendship lasted for six years. They promised each other that when they were older they would marry and have children. They were not put off by my insistence that having children normally needed a man and a woman: 'That's no problem, Dad. We'll use a sperm bank!' But when primary school finished they went to different secondary schools where new friendships were established and old ones forgotten. Children are just as capable as adults of forming meaningful relationships with each other, and just as vulnerable when these relationships fail. They can also be fairly fickle with friendships and you're likely to find that if they lose a friendship, however traumatic it might seem in that moment, it will not be long before they find their feet with new companions.

If the course of your child's friendships do not run smoothly, witnessing those friendships fail or seeing your child miserable because they're not part of the 'in' group can cause parents a great deal of anxiety. If your child is nursing a broken heart, think back to when you were the same age and try to be sympathetic, recognise their emotions and reassure them that their feelings are normal. Although we may think that making friends as a child comes naturally, like all of us they have to work at it, and for some children this can be a difficult, scary and worrying prospect. Shyness, lack of confidence and, sometimes, just plain selfishness can stand in the way of your child developing satisfying friendships, but there are things you can do as a parent to help smooth the inevitable ups and downs of children's friendships. For instance, if difficult friendships are causing a problem, then it is not always helpful to ban your child from staying close to the 'problem' friend, since it gives them the message that their judgement is not to be trusted. Trying to forbid these friendships will only strengthen them, especially if your child is at an age when rebellion is quite natural, but it's a good idea to help them start nurturing other friendships with more mature, kindly children. Make suggestions which help reduce the amount of time your child spends with the difficult friend out of school time. Explain that everyone has the freedom to choose how they behave and who they're friends with, and that it is not wrong to simply walk away from situations that are upsetting or difficult.

If you were to ask me what I feared most for my two daughters – serious illness and harm aside – it would have been lack of friendships and unhappiness at school. Like most parents I wanted my children to be happy and to make friends (which I still do), which means, of course, finding ways to deal with being left out of a conversation, classroom cliques, friendship breakdowns, and mean or bullying children. Sadly, it is almost inevitable that children will experience some or all of these problems as they get older and especially in the turbulent years of adolescence. What can you do to help them navigate successfully through such challenges?

In general, girls tend to have more complex friendship problems than boys. This is because, while boys can bully by hitting, grabbing, pushing and so on, girls mostly exercise relationship bullying: excluding a girl from a group, calling her names, spreading rumours, etc. You have to be careful in situations like this that your own buttons aren't being pushed and that you aren't yourself getting dragged into a response that's too emotional. Instead, encourage your daughter into a mix of friendships that are wider than her peer group – older or younger children, aunties and grandparents, so that the peer group influence is less. And staying close to the same sex parent is also important for both boys and girls who are having friendship problems. It means that they have a safe harbour to go to.

If, on the other hand, rather than being bullied your child is having difficulty making friends, then suggest having someone over for tea after school, or try to make contact with other parents whose children you like so that it becomes natural for your child to be friendly with theirs. If they find friendships generally difficult, try joining them up with activities that will keep them busy and naturally around other children who they might relate to away from their school life. Encourage your child to demonstrate kindness in front of other children, for instance, by including other left-out children in their activity. For children who are still learning how to get along, it can be helpful to plan what to do before having a friend over for a play date. This could involve deciding whether to share all of their toys or only some, or encouraging them to think about what games the other child would like to play when they arrive. Observe your child to work out the negative social behaviours your child uses too often and the positive social behaviours they could use more. Little things, such as smiles, looking at the person, knowing names and using a confident, friendly voice can make a big difference when making friends. Friendships require give and take. By sharing toys, time, games, experiences and feelings, children learn that they can have their social needs met and can meet the needs of others. Since friendships develop through this kind of mutual exchange, close friendships are usually based on well-matched needs. So are your children moving among children somewhat like them, with similar interests and 'ways of operating'?

Talking to your children about their friends is important. For instance, talk to your child, of whatever age, about controlling negative emotions and paying attention to the needs and wants of others. Whether or not there are friendship problems, it is helpful to ask them about their friendships, and to ask them to reflect on how they feel about their different friends. And if there are difficulties then talking problems through with a supportive adult helps children to think about what is happening and why, how they feel about it, and what to do next. Thinking things through like this helps to build more mature social skills.

Children's friendship needs and skills change as they grow. Similarly, children's ideas about friendship change as they develop. This is partly reflected in the different kinds of activities that children like to spend time doing with their friends at different ages. The table below (taken from an Australian government publication) indicates the ways children tend to describe close friends and the kinds of skills that support positive friendships as they develop.

Approximate age	A friend is someone who...	Friendship skills include...
Up to 1 year		· Looking, smiling, touching, imitating
1–2 years	· Plays with you · Has good toys · Can do fun things	· Identifying friend by name
3–5 years	· Does something that pleases you · You know better than other people	· Playing well in a twosome · Approaching others to join in
5–7 years	· Helps and looks after you · You help	· Taking others' feelings into account · Seeing others' viewpoint
8–10 years	· Plays fair – follows the rules · Talks and shares interests	· Talking and listening to each other · Forming groups with similar interests
10–12 years	· Trusts you and is trustworthy	· Sharing confidences · Negotiating · Respecting one another
12–18 years	· Understands you and who you understand · You can talk to about feelings or problems	· Talking about personal and social issues · Supporting one another

Most children will go through friendship conflicts and difficulties, and although they might seem dramatic at the time, it is rare for these difficulties to cause any long-lasting psychological damage. Even children who are usually popular experience rejection sometimes. When this happens children's confidence may be affected and they may blame themselves. Beliefs about the reasons for the friendship conflicts they experience affect the ways that children react. Some kinds of thinking are more helpful than others for managing the conflicts that children have with friends. If you make yourself aware of the positive social skills which your child might demonstrate to reduce friendship problems then you are in a much better position to help them.

Poor social skills are shown in these behaviours: being 'rough' and physically aggressive, being a poor loser, arguing and getting into others' space, interrupting and talking over others, name calling, taking others' possessions and showing off.

On the other hand, positive social skills are shown in these behaviours: sharing, taking turns, asking for what one needs, apologising to others, following the rules of the game, complimenting and listening to others, cooperating and refusing to join in others' negative behaviours.

Children who are good at making and keeping friends use positive social skills. Parents can help children learn these positive social skills by guiding them, offering positive examples for them to follow and providing opportunities for play where children can practise their friendship skills. The key social skills that help with friendships include such things as ability to cooperate and communicate clearly, empathy (understanding how others are feeling), emotional control and taking responsibility. These skills are possible to learn. Teaching compassion and empathy in friendship situations, however, needs modelling. As in most parenting situations you have to practise what you preach. It isn't helpful for your child to hear you gossiping or saying unpleasant things about your own friends or other parents. It is helpful for a child when a parent supports them to solve friendship conflicts by encouraging resilient, cooperative attitudes. Rather than simply blaming the other children the adult may say something like, 'What else can you do? Are there other children who might be interested in playing a game?'

Real-life friendship problems come in all forms, some of which you will consider trivial, but it won't help your child to minimise the problem. While it is tempting to reassure your child that not being invited to a party isn't the end of the world, it is better to acknowledge that, in their world at least, it is the cause of serious worry. If your child is having problems with their friends, don't tell them not to worry, or to get over it, or to grow up and be sensible, or simply just to try to get along with people. Instead, let them see that you are taking their concerns seriously while also helping them to look at the matter with some perspective: 'You haven't been invited. That must feel bad, I understand.' Don't, on the other hand, show anger and upset on their behalf. You are likely then simply to amplify their negative feelings. Try to remain calm even if what they are telling you is upsetting for you too. And remember that, even though you can see the issues clearly, and have years of wisdom and experience in human relations that they lack, you can't fix their problems with other people. They have to find a way of doing that. Listen, talk things through, ask pertinent questions. Do more listening than talking. Follow their story rather than telling them yours. For instance, ask about whether it is ignoring or challenging behaviour that is the cause of the problem. Even if they don't immediately figure things out it will be a reassurance for them to know they have been heard and understood. If though the problem becomes really serious and is leading to anxiety, lack of sleep or signs of depression, then it is entirely legitimate to intervene and to discuss the matter with their teacher or other parent or relevant adult.

It is worth knowing that the biggest group in any class is 'the bystanders' – children who are neutral in any dispute but who can really help children who are being picked on or left out. Teach your children to be kind and compassionate and they are more likely to be able to build alliances with this large middle group when problems arise. One good thing to do is to encourage your child to use their internal moral compass – the instrument we all have inside of us telling us when things just aren't right, the gut instinct we have for what is right and what is wrong, the inner ear, which lets us know when something makes us feel uncomfortable. For instance, your child might feel uncomfortable about party games or sleepovers, or uncomfortable about stroking animals. Tell them that this is OK – it's just their internal 'self' telling them what is right for them. So you can from time to time say, 'Does this feel right for you?' or 'Does this feel safe and comfortable for you?' Then if they encounter difficult or nasty attitudes or actions in others they will have the tools to say no and walk away.

One of my saviours when I was ten years old was a boy called John Saunders. My primary school was quite a rough school in a West London suburb, and there were bullies in my class always looking for fights after school. They would pick on other pupils they knew were less physically strong, knowing that they would be the victor. I fell into the potential victim group. I didn't really fit in with the big, bad boys, but John Saunders was my ally; we played together at weekends and seemed to understand each other. We supported each other when we talked about the inevitable challenges that came our way from the bullies. I never saw John Saunders after primary school, but I remember his name and his friendship over fifty years later. It is very important for children to have these kinds of friendships, or perhaps a cousin or older sibling, outside of the school cliques, who they know they can rely on. So this is another reason for encouraging your child to have interests outside of school where they can make different kinds of friendships from those that are made in the enclosed school environment. As well as helping them to build different talents and interests, it will build confidence, the kind of confidence you need to overcome difficult times, and it will put playground troubles into perspective and give them someone to turn to.

Parents do have an important role to play in helping children develop friendships. They set examples for children to follow the ways in which they manage relationships. They can model the right phrases for children to use in conflict situations. They can act as coaches for children, teaching them helpful social skills and talking through friendship issues to help with solving problems. As they learn how to manage social situations, having opportunities to talk about friendships with parents helps children feel supported and develops their communication skills. Teach one behaviour or social skill at a time and make sure the child is able to use it before introducing another skill. Show your child what to do. You may act out the situation and even demonstrate what to say. Take turns 'acting' until your child can demonstrate what to do. But don't be too serious; make it a fun experience. This kind of coaching is critical for helping children use new skills in real-life situations. Coaching involves prompting, reminding and encouraging (but not nagging!) children to use the skills they have learned. Coach your child to practise positive social skills in everyday situations with family members and friends and it might surprise you what a difference it makes to your child's social confidence.

So what else can we as parents do to make sure that our children grow up knowing how to make good friends? Well, if there is more than one child in the family, then learning to get on with your sibling is a good lesson in how to make good friendships.

Acknowledge, first of all though, that your children are likely to have very different personalities, which might affect how close they are when older. My own daughters were very close when younger, the oldest used to help the youngest get dressed, and they played together very happily until their early teens when academic competition kicked in and they were very keen do 'outdo' each other at school. They are now, as adults, very different people and still very good friends but inevitably not as close as they were when they lived under the same roof and played with the same toys. The trick for a parent is to make each feel good about themselves and their particular skills and abilities, rather than inadequate because one doesn't have the talents the other has. The relationship between siblings is bound to be intense when they spend so much time together, but if you nurture 'the good bits' in each, there is less likelihood of jealousy and the feeling that parents prefer one or the other. At the same time do things as a family that are cooperative and help 'team-building' to give them a natural opportunity to support each other – in my case it was putting up tents on camping holidays! You might also want to set up a schedule which outlines who gets to do what on which days. This will start to remind the other sibling to take their turn. Importantly, don't ever leap in to blame one child, normally the eldest, if something has gone wrong. That child is likely to complain, 'It's always me who gets told off.' Ask yourself if there is any truth in this. Sometimes we criticise children because they are displaying the same traits we wish we could get rid of in ourselves, and sometimes we criticise children simply because they are very different to us. If you get caught up in the 'she hit me; no I didn't' scenario, then say: 'I don't know who did what, so we are moving on now,' but if you do see one sibling being horrid to another, say something like: 'I saw you being unkind just then but I know that is not like you. How can you be kind again?' Go back to values rather than casting blame. Always criticise the act, not the person, and if you find it difficult to give each sibling equal attention share out the responsibility with your partner or a relative.

In childhood, friends are mostly other children who are fun to play with. During young adulthood, friendships become more complex and meaningful. In adolescence, there's a lot more self-disclosure and support between friends, but adolescents are still discovering their identity, and learning what it means to be intimate. Their friendships help them do that. For adults, in the hierarchy of relationships friendships are at the bottom – romantic partners, husbands/wives, parents and children normally come first. Children have, naturally, a smaller circle of relationships and in this circle friendships are crucially important to them. Friendships are unique relationships because unlike family relationships, we *choose* to enter into them, and survey upon survey shows how important children's friends are to their happiness. The special thing about friendship is that friends are friends because they want to be; that friends choose each other is a 'double jeopardy' though, because you can choose to get in, and you can also choose to get out. Still, throughout life, from nursery school to the retirement home, friendship continues to confer health benefits, both mental and physical, and so it is incumbent on parents to help children learn how to build friendships, a skill that will convey benefits throughout their life. So, take care of your child's friendships. In fact, if your child is old enough, you could show them this quote from a Quaker missionary and pin it up in their bedroom somewhere:

I expect to pass through life but once. If therefore there can be any kindness I can show, or any good thing I can do to a fellow being, let me do it now, and do not defer or neglect it, as I shall not pass this way again.

(Stephen Grellet 1773–1855)

YOU SHALL HONOUR DISCIPLINE

Discipline is necessary in every family. The goal of discipline is not to punish but to teach, to help children choose acceptable behaviours and learn self-control. Your child may test the limits you establish for them, but they need those limits to grow into a responsible adult. There is a saying in moral philosophy that the palace of reason is entered through the courtyard of habit.

Let's start with the obvious. Any discipline worth acquiring cannot be beaten into anyone. Children do not need to be hit to learn an important lesson. Physical punishment does not work and is, in any case, illegal. Virtually all child development experts now assert that strong punishment does not work. In particular, spanking teaches children that it's OK to hit when they're angry. It can physically harm children and rather than teaching children how to change·

their behaviour it makes them fearful of their parents and merely teaches them to avoid getting caught. For children seeking attention by misbehaviour, spanking may paradoxically 'reward' them – negative attention is better than no attention at all. This is not to say, of course, that you should not exert your authority. Of course you should. Ground rules and boundaries, with sanctions if they are broken, are essential if your child is to accept reasonable authority. Perhaps express severe disappointment to a child, perhaps send them to their room to be on their own for a period, but correcting a child with threats of force and strict punishments lowers self-respect and does not encourage growth as an independent person.

Self-discipline, based on parental modelling, is the most effective discipline. Parents can be quiet and logical messengers of appropriate behaviour simply by demonstrating patience and self-discipline themselves. I have seen this demonstrated very clearly while living in The Netherlands – a country rated by Unicef as the best for quality of life for children. It is very rare to see a toddler screaming or crying in public. In many countries when this does happen the parent, getting agitated, bends down and threatens the child, or shouts at them to stop. In The Netherlands you will see, on the rare occasions when you see a child crying out loud in a supermarket or shop, the parent, often the father, simply kneels down beside them, and talks to try to calm them, without raising their voice or making a fuss. The effect is usually quite fast. The parent, in demonstrating quiet and assured behaviour in the face of stress, demonstrates to the child how they might cope with a stressful or anxious situation, and the child follows their lead. Tantrums are developmentally normal. All young children have them. Older children should not, but if you do what your child wants simply because 'they will freak out if I don't' then you are doing your child no favours. It is more helpful if parents disentangle themselves from the trap the child has drawn them into. The key is to remain both consistent and calm, and even as I write that I realise how difficult it is in the moment. One way to do this is to try to keep a sense of humour to reduce tension in situations. If you gently bounce a baby on your knee and it is sick down your best suit, there is no point in being angry about it and shouting at the baby. You have to gently bounce, gurn or sing to the baby, but at all costs you must stay calm and in charge of the baby who is in your care. Rewarding bad behaviour by giving it attention through shouting or arguing is likely to encourage the child to behave badly more often. If you ignore it, or there is a negative consequence, they will stop doing it.

Discipline should be about teaching acceptable behaviour rather than punishing children for doing something wrong. There is a Dutch saying: 'What the old cock crows, the young cock learns.' In other words, adults are expected to set a good example for children to follow. Children mimic their parents. So, for instance, you can model social skills to help your child get on in the world: eye contact, positive body language, good manners and consistency are all good signals to your child about how to interact well with others. On the other hand, talking on your phone at a restaurant or café table is not. But you can be very firm and straightforward at the same time. Do not ask children to do something, but simply tell them, giving clear directions rather than a set of options: 'I want you to...', 'You must...' And sometimes it is OK to make your child wait. Don't rush to replace their phone the minute it is broken or give them what they want to avoid a tantrum. When it comes to family discipline, patience is a virtue and an essential skill.

I have said that correcting a child with threats of force and strict punishments does not work, but the opposite is equally true. If you are struggling to say 'No!' when that is necessary, then perhaps you are more interested in being a friend of your child than their parent. It is often a good idea to operate as a school does, where children understand the rules and the consequences of poor behaviour. Good schools give children a lot of attention for good behaviour but very little for behaviour which is disapproved of. Children in most schools, at least good ones, know where they stand. You can be assertive and clear with children of all ages without being a strict disciplinarian. You can set clear boundaries without damaging your relationship with your child. In fact, clear boundaries can help that relationship. You see everywhere parents who are frightened to do this: in obese children, in children tired because they go to bed too late or children who are allowed to watch TV programmes/films and play video games, which are not appropriate for their age. Why do parents feel they must negotiate, compromise, bribe? You can communicate simply and clearly with your child: 'You cannot do this. I'm sorry, no'; 'You know that is not good for you. You will not do it'; 'If you continue to act like that, this will happen until you change.' Of course, you should hold reasoning conversations with children when they are older, but too much discussion especially with younger children reinforces the problem by giving it attention. Start with boundaries and consistent messages. There is something reassuring about routine, structure and boundaries for children.

Remember, the palace of reason has to be entered through the courtyard of habit. Without consistent messages and clear boundaries, the child ends up perplexed. Do my parents mean it or not?

Of course, as children get older you have to find a way to make them see for themselves what is right and what is wrong. When I was a teacher-training student I remember going to a tutor, who was a gruff Yorkshireman, with my lesson plans for a teaching practice. I was looking for a discussion, perhaps some advice on how to improve things, perhaps one or two helpful tips, but he simply said, 'It's rubbish. Go away and do it again.' So I said, 'But what's wrong?' 'You work it out, lad,' was his reply. Seeing him some years later I thought I'd politely get my own back so I told him, 'You were a really difficult tutor – you gave me so little advice or guidance.' 'Aye, son, but I gave you something much more valuable. I helped you to think for yourself didn't I?' So one challenge for parents as their children get older is this: once your child reaches the doors of the palace of reason, are you teaching them to be responsible for themselves, or dependent on you? All children will gain a sense of well-being and self-esteem when they are encouraged to take responsibility for themselves.

So how exactly do you keep a one year old from putting their fingers in the electric socket? What should you do when your preschooler throws a tantrum? How can you get a teenager to respect your parental authority? The answer is that whatever your child's age, it's important to be consistent when it comes to discipline. If parents don't stick to the rules and consequences they set up, their children aren't likely to either. Here are some ideas about how to vary your approach to discipline to best fit your family and the age of your child, from toddlers to teens:

- Babies and toddlers are naturally curious, so it's wise to eliminate temptations – items, such as TVs and video equipment, stereos, jewellery, mobile phones and especially cleaning supplies and medicines, should be kept well out of reach. When your crawling baby or roving toddler heads towards an unacceptable or dangerous object, calmly say 'No' and either remove your child from the area or distract him or her with an appropriate activity.

- For toddlers, timeouts can be effective discipline. A child who has been hitting or throwing food, for example, should be told why the behaviour is unacceptable and taken to a designated timeout area – a kitchen chair or bottom stair – for a minute or two to calm down (longer timeouts are not effective for toddlers). Don't forget that children learn by watching adults, particularly their parents. Make sure your behaviour is role model material. You'll make a much stronger impression by putting your own belongings away rather than just issuing orders to your child to pick up toys while your stuff is left strewn around.

- As your child grows and begins to understand the connection between actions and consequences, make sure you start communicating the rules of your family's home. For preschoolers explain what you expect of them *before* you punish them for a certain behaviour. For instance, the first time your three year old uses crayons to decorate the living room wall, discuss why that's not allowed and what will happen if your child does it again (for instance, your child will have to help clean the wall and will not be able to use the crayons for the rest of the day). If the wall gets decorated again a few days later, issue a reminder that crayons are for paper only and then enforce the consequences. The earlier that parents establish this kind of 'I set the rules and you're expected to listen or accept the consequences' standard, the better for everyone. Although it's sometimes easier for parents to ignore occasional bad behaviour or not follow through on some threatened punishment, this sets a bad precedent. Consistency is the key to effective discipline, and it's important for parents to decide (together, if you are not a single parent) what the rules are and then uphold them.

- Don't forget to reward good behaviour. Don't underestimate the positive effect that your positive reinforcement can have – discipline is not just about punishment but more about recognising and acknowledging good behaviour. For example, saying 'I'm proud of you for sharing your toys at playgroup' is usually more effective than punishing a child who didn't share. Be specific when giving praise rather than just saying 'Well done!' It's important to tell children what the right thing to do is, not just to say what the wrong thing is. For example, instead of saying 'Don't jump on the sofa,' try, 'Please sit properly on the sofa and put your feet on the floor not on the cushions.'

- If your child continues an unacceptable behaviour no matter what you do, try making a chart with a box for each day of the week. Decide how many times your child can misbehave before a punishment kicks in or how long the proper behaviour must be seen before it is rewarded. Post the chart on the fridge and then track the good and unacceptable behaviours every day. This will give your child (and you) a concrete look at how it's going. Once this begins to work, praise your child for learning to control misbehaviour and, especially, for overcoming any stubborn problem.

- Timeouts can also work well for children at any age. Pick a suitable timeout place that's free of distractions so your child will have time to think about how he or she has behaved – getting sent to your room isn't effective if a computer, TV or games are there. Be sure to consider the length of time that will work best for your child. Experts say one minute for each year of age is a good rule of thumb; others recommend using the timeout until the child has calmed down (to teach self-regulation). Again, consistency is crucial, as is follow-through. Make good on any promises of discipline or else you risk undermining your authority. Children have to believe that you mean what you say. This is not to say you can't give second chances or allow a certain margin of error, but for the most part, you should act on what you say.

- Be careful not to make unrealistic threats of punishment ('Slam that door and you'll never play on your computer again!') in anger, since not following through could weaken *all* your threats. If you threaten to turn the car around and go home if the squabbling in the back seat doesn't stop, make sure you do exactly that. The credibility you'll gain with your children is much more valuable than losing a day out at the theme park.

- As children approach the teenage years – just as with all ages – they can be disciplined with natural consequences. As they mature and request more independence and responsibility, teaching them to deal with the consequences of their behaviour is an effective and appropriate method of discipline. Very severe sanctions though may take away your power as a parent. If you forbid your son or daughter any outings for a month, your child may not feel motivated to change their behaviour because everything has already been taken away. For example, if your eleven year old's homework isn't done before bedtime, should you make him or her stay up to do it or even lend a hand yourself? Probably not – you'll miss an opportunity to teach a key life lesson. If homework is incomplete, your child will go to school the next day without it and suffer the resulting bad grade. It's natural for parents to want to rescue children from mistakes, but in the long run they do children a favour by letting them fail sometimes. Children see what behaving improperly can mean and probably won't make those mistakes again.

- Once your child reaches the teenage years you have laid the foundations. Your child knows what is right and wrong, knows what is expected of them and that you mean what you say about the penalties for bad behaviour. Don't let your guard down! Discipline is just as important for teens as it is for younger children. Just as with the four year old who needs you to set a bedtime and enforce it, your teenager needs boundaries too.

- For the family to work smoothly there have to be rules regarding homework, visits by friends, curfews, dating, etc. and discuss them beforehand with your teenager so there will be no misunderstandings. Your teen will probably complain from time to time, but also will realise that you're in control. Believe it or not, teens still want and need you to set limits and enforce order in their lives, even as you grant them greater freedom and responsibility.

- When your teenager does break a rule, taking away privileges may seem the best plan of action. While it's fine to take away pocket money for a week, for example, be sure to also explain and discuss why coming home an hour past the agreed time is unacceptable and worrisome. On the other hand, remember to give a teenager some control over things. Not only will this limit the number of power struggles you have, it will help your teen respect the decisions that you do need to make. You could allow a younger teenager to make decisions concerning weekend clothes, hairstyles or even the condition of his or her room, and as they get older, that realm of control can gradually be extended.

- Walk older children through their decision-making processes that take into consideration people who could be affected. For example, if your child wants to quit a sport or other activity, encourage them to identify the source of the problem and consider their commitment to the team. Then help them figure out if giving up does, in fact, fix the problem.

- Studies show that people who engage in the habit of expressing gratitude are more likely to be helpful, generous, compassionate and forgiving – and they're also more likely to be happy and healthy. So it's fine for parents to insist on children helping out around the house, and to ask children to help their siblings. Simply give them thanks when they have completed a task or helpful action.

Every time a child moves on to the next stage in life, from nursery to primary school, from primary school to secondary school, into puberty, taking exams, changing friendships, you might see them regress emotionally and in confidence a little at first and then seem to surge forwards, stretching the boundaries you have carefully put in place for them. Your child might change friends, want to try new ways of dressing and want to stay up later in the evenings. Don't assume these are rejections of you. They are explorations and discoveries. Even so, accepting this new behaviour is not to diminish the need for personal and family boundaries. Boundaries are like belts that can be extended a notch or two to accommodate growth. Your boundaries around bedtime may get stretched, but there will still be a boundary, and you will still be firm with other boundaries – not taking risks, not talking rudely to adults and other behaviours which are unacceptable to you. If your child is now a teenager, don't be too quick to give in to a clash of opinions. A teenager's immature brain is unable to cope with too much responsibility if it is handed to them too soon. In fact, the prefrontal cortex of the brain – the part that determines personality, moderation of social behaviour and decision-making – is only fully formed in females at twenty and in males at twenty-four years of age. Your teenager's loud music and purple hair are not there to drive you mad; they are signs of their developing personality trying to build an identity. Radical hair, clothing and music might seem to you rebellious, but they are essentially harmless. I drew a line with tattoos, forbidding my daughters to get one until they were over eighteen, using the rule: 'You can't do anything to your body that is difficult to undo.' You will have your own 'line in the sand' and that's as it should be, so long as it is clearly explained to your child.

Nonetheless it does little good to cling to rules and punishments in a desperate attempt to keep control. However difficult it is letting go of the reins, resist the urge to always wade in and insist you are right. Teenagers especially can make adults act like teenagers – but you have a fully developed brain, remember. If you do lose your cool, apologise. Nothing warms a child's heart more than an adult owning up to their own imperfections. The teenage years are a developmental journey for both parents and children, and parents have to 'hang in there' during their transition to adulthood. So, for instance, never go to war over schoolwork, which is often a cause of stress between teenagers and parents. It is impossible to make a child of any age learn if they do not want to. Concentrate instead on strategies which shift the way a child thinks from 'my parent wants me to do this' to 'I should do this for myself'. Just don't make excuses for your child if they fail to hand in homework or get into trouble at school. The child has to understand the consequences of their actions, whether good or bad, and shielding them from negative consequences will not help them get into good habits. You can make life easier though by setting up a process and a structure for homework. Does your child have a good working environment, free of distractions, a reasonable writing surface and access to a computer if they need it? Do you encourage them to make a start with their homework, and let them know when the expected time of completion is up? Helping can mean simply being aware of how much homework is set, helping your child to plan ahead and manage the different tasks, and letting them know when they are running over the allotted time. Some schools encourage this kind of help by setting up homework diaries which teacher, student and parent all have to sign. Not getting involved at all is as unhelpful as helicoptering over your child's homework. It can reduce confidence and motivation if parents seldom show interest. Structure your help so that children understand that they are getting support and advice, but make it less specific and less frequent as the child gets older and gains the ability to carry out the homework without any adult intervention. Perhaps think of yourself as a teaching assistant, providing nuggets of advice or coaching, but never think of yourself as the teacher – children will have spent the school day with teachers. It's not great if they return home to find a parent acting in this role also.

One small trick can make a huge difference to the relationship you have with your child. That trick is to catch them being good! Notice things they do rather than things they don't. Have you ever stopped to think about how many times you react negatively to your children in a given day? Take a check on yourself one day. You may be surprised to find out how often you criticise rather than compliment. How would you feel about a friend who treated you with that much negative guidance, even if it was well intentioned? The more effective approach is to catch your child doing something right: 'You've made your bed every day this week without being asked – that's terrific!' or 'I was watching you play with your sister and you were very patient, despite the fact that she was difficult.' These statements will do more to encourage good behaviour over the long run than repeated reprimand. But do remember the second commandment! When it comes to rewarding 'good' behaviour, the experts recommend that parents only praise uncommon acts of kindness or generosity or thoughtfulness, rather than everyday good behaviour that should be the norm. Of course, you want your children to be successful in life, to achieve their goals, but researchers believe that doesn't have to come at the expense of kindness and empathy. In fact, children who are encouraged to be morally upstanding can also be goals-oriented humans and gain the happiness you want them to have.

Recently, in schools at least, 'mindfulness' has started to play a part in creating disciplined children. Mindfulness is the idea that paying attention to the present moment and letting go of negative thoughts is good for you. The idea started being used by big corporations, universities, the military and even prisons. Mindfulness for children is a relatively recent development but is certainly gaining traction – increasing numbers of head teachers are implementing the practice in schools. Private classes for children are springing up too, claiming benefits including increasing children's attention span and their ability to calm themselves when upset, and reducing anxiety. Getting children to lie down and make up stories together, take part in yoga sessions or listen to meditation downloads (e.g. from audible. co.uk) are all variations of this theme of quietening your mind and learning to concentrate. Books with titles such as *The Art of Mindfulness for Children* and *Sitting Still Like a Frog* are increasingly being found on bookshelves. And teenage apps, such as 'Smiling Mind' and 'Take a Chill', are also selling well. Mindfulness might seem like a new fad but its main elements can be seen in many religious disciplines, and the notion has the intellectual stamp of approval. Willem Kuyken, Professor of Clinical Psychology at Oxford University, is reported to have said (*Sunday Telegraph* 13/3/16) that 'the spread of mindfulness among children could do for mental health what fluoride did for teeth'. So perhaps if your child seems to lack control in some aspects of their life, it might be worth exploring these resources.

The idea of being in the moment comes naturally to preschoolers, but a part of mindfulness is about observing our own thoughts and using that reflection to decide how to react. Young children have not yet achieved this meta-cognitive ability, but there are things they can do in this vein. Exercises you might try with younger children include 'stop, drop and breathe', where a child getting stressed can try to diffuse it by dropping to the floor and concentrating on their breathing. Then there are 'breathing buddies', where the child has a designated soft toy they place on their tummy and watch it move up and down when they breathe in and out. Anything that helps children to become kinder and calmer is surely to be welcomed, but mindfulness isn't some kind of golden bullet to 'cure' discipline problems.

It is somewhat ironic, of course, that a lot of parents wanting to fill their children with calmness are also filling their children's schedules to the maximum with extra maths, music and sports. The striving mentality endemic in society, which might create success, is also sometimes the cause of mental health issues in children. Preferable surely is to have a lifestyle where there is time outdoors in nature, and for activities that don't necessarily have an obvious goal except to enjoy life. Think back to being the parent of a toddler on a picnic. You sit on a picnic rug and the food is laid out in front of you. You have drinks and sun hats ready, umbrellas too. Balls and other toys have come with you. To start with your toddler stays close on the rug, but then they see something that catches their curiosity and they toddle off a short distance. As they gain confidence they move further and further away, but from time to time they return to the rug for reassurance. Your job is to keep an eye on them.

If they go out of sight you will stand up and move to where you can see them. If there are dangers, such as a river or a road, you will certainly tell them not to go near. If they suddenly see a dog which frightens them they might rush back to the rug and into your arms. Sometimes when you see them playing with other toddlers a little way away you might feel a pang of loneliness sitting there on your own. Soon though they return and ask you to come to see the amazing discovery they have made. You go with them and listen to them tell you all about it. It is their adventure after all. This is the picture to keep in mind when you think about your child's development, well-being and behaviour. Certainly there will be 'wobbles' and points when you will despair that they will ever 'grow up' into mature adults, but soon enough they will leave you to set up their own home, and before that they may stay away for longer periods than you are comfortable with. Don't be surprised if they return for a hug and emotional support when there are wobbles in their life. If you have kept the sixth commandment – You shall honour discipline – your children will be independent and thoughtful individuals, but they will also want to know where you are, even when they are far away.

REMEMBER LITERACY TO KEEP IT HOLY

Being able to read is an essential part of being able to thrive as an adult in the modern world. Finding the best way to inspire children to become fluent readers has long been debated by governments and educationalists. The 'look and say' method, where children learned to memorise words, dominated in the 1940s, 50s and 60s, and then the pendulum swung towards phonics-based teaching, where children decode words by sounds. The debate rages on among teachers and academics. So how is a parent to know what is best for their child in this area? How do you help a child learn to turn those strange marks and shapes on the page into meaning? Learning to read is not easy, yet you are reading this book, so clearly you managed it! The mystery of reading is wonderfully captured in this extract from a letter written by the English novelist

Daniel Defoe in 1727. He recounts with amazement how a young reader is able to make instantaneous translation from one form of words to another in order to make sense of what he is reading:

> *I sat down by the Master, till the boy had read it out, and observed that the boy read a little oddly in the Tone of the Country, which made me the more attentive; because on Inquiry, I found that the words were the same and the Orthography the same, as in all our Bibles. I observed also the Boy read it out with his Eyes still on the book and his Head, like a mere Boy, moving from Side to Side, as the lines reached across the Columns of the book … the words were these:*
>
> *"I have put off my Coat; how shall I put it on? I have washed my feet; how shall I defile them?"*
>
> *The Boy read thus, with his Eyes, as I say, full on the text:*
>
> *"Chav a duffed me coot, how shall I don't; Chav a washed me feet; how shall I muff 'em?"*
>
> *How the dextrous Dunce could form his Mouth to express so readily the Words (which stood right printed in the Book) in his Country Jargon, I could not but admire.*

(Quoted in Moyle 1977)

Most parents of good readers have no idea how they contribute to their children becoming good readers, but you should take comfort from the fact that across many countries and cultures and using a variety of methods, the vast majority of human beings, particularly in the Western world, manage to acquire the ability to read. So the chances of your child becoming literate are very high … whatever you do! When I asked one parent of a fluent reader what they had done to encourage her, he said, 'Not a single thing!' Of course, he couldn't be right; he simply had done things he wasn't aware of doing – reading to his daughter and filling the house with books. What he meant was, he didn't plan it; he didn't actually instruct his child in reading. Your parents will have similarly helped you almost without knowing they were teaching you to read: teaching you the alphabet; drawing your attention to simple words that you could remember – 'the', 'go', 'and', 'run'; asking you to write your name and label things; helping you to make words on the fridge out of plastic letters perhaps; reading stories and rhymes to you and repeating them from time to time; helping you to see the storyline in simple 'beginning reading' books; telling you the sound at the start of a word so you could 'attack' it.

You learned to read, but some find it difficult and a few can't read at all. Those children almost certainly didn't gain an understanding of the fact that letters make sounds and that most, but by no means all, letters and letter combinations make the same sounds over and over again (the linguist David Crystal estimates that eighty per cent of English words are phonetically regular, but the other twenty per cent contain many of the most common words in English, such as the first word in many traditional children's stories, 'Once upon a time'). For these children what is usually called 'phonics', a method where children learn systematically the letter combinations which make particular sounds, has been found to be the most useful in teaching them to read. But a system that works for some may not be the best for everyone. Teachers know that most children learn to read using a variety of methods and are usually pragmatic about this. Most parents will understand this too. Children do not all learn in the same way. Different children learn better from different activities depending on their strengths and interests. Too strong a focus on one particular method will deny a child the variety of strategies that anyone needs to be able to read fluently. Of course, since reading is an important educational achievement the more effectively children are taught to read the better, but often when this is said, people mean by teaching reading and decoding letters into words and words into sentences. They mean teaching children the rules of letters and sounds. However, started too early this can be entirely counterproductive and turn children off reading. Learning to read will be useless if children don't actually want to read. Rather think of 'start early' as introducing children to nursery rhymes and showing them picture books. Reading begins at home not with formal teaching but with children eagerly listening to stories, which make them sit up and take notice, giggle and ask questions.

The best course of action with reading, as with many other things, is to consider your child first, rather than any particular method, to see how they react to different methods and ways of understanding a book, and to follow what seems to be the most successful. Most important of all, of course, is to encourage your child to read for meaning and want to read more and more now and for the rest of their lives. Some of the world's most beautiful, funny and amazing books have been written for children. One of the joys of childhood, and parenthood, is discovering such books. If a child learns to read for pleasure they are equipping themselves with one of the major attributes they will need to be successful in life. The 2009 Programme for International Student Assessment study showed that in all countries students who enjoy reading most and who read in their own time for enjoyment perform across all subjects significantly better than students who enjoy reading the least (OECD 2010).

I was shocked recently to hear a conversation between a father and his two boys in a department store. Two young boys, probably about six and seven, obviously brothers, walked past me heading for the colourful and inviting children's book section. They shouted back at their dad, 'Over here, Dad, can we go and look at the books.' His reply, 'No, come on you two. You'll never read them anyway!' And yet we know that children who own no books at home tend to enjoy reading less and rate themselves as less confident readers, but their reading level is raised when given self-chosen books.

Whatever the state of the educational debate about learning to read, experts all agree that one of the key factors for children is the status of reading at home. When children have a family where reading and talking about books is part of their world, where the culture of reading is an everyday part of family life, this helps to produce better readers. In homes where this is not the case, then introducing children to the pleasure of reading books becomes one of the most important jobs teachers have to do. Of course, children need to develop the skill, but they also need to develop the will to read. Motivating and inspiring their child to read, and being a good reading role model, can be a most important task. And we know that children with good oral language skills and good general knowledge are likely to become good readers, so simply talking to your child about the things that interest them, and introducing them to new vocabulary through new experiences, is also helping them form the base of knowledge about language they will need to be able to read fluently. How, for instance, has a child any chance of reading the word 'autumn', if they have no idea about the concept of the seasons?

Reading regularly to children from an early age is crucially important. If you are read to at an early age by someone you love, then you will in turn learn to love stories and books. Make reading part of an everyday routine so children quickly pick up subtle skills, such as when to turn a page, how to follow the print of a book from left to right, how to use pictures to help decode words, and how to recognise initial letters of commonly used words. It's good to let children see adults reading too, not just books but magazines, newspapers, Kindles and iPads. Children learn by copying. Parents can share the stories they are reading or any funny or interesting nuggets they come across that they think will spark their child's interest. And let children read what interests them, whether that's comics, or football books, or magazines, or screen texts, so they realise that reading is fun. The other key building block which parents of young children can help put in place is a familiarity with rhymes and different word sounds. Singing and chanting poems and nursery rhymes to children will help them to learn their favourites and decipher rhyming words and different sounds, all of which will help them with their phonic skills later on. If children receive all this informal help and support at home before they start school, this is far more likely to be helpful than formal instruction.

The father of a very competent three year old I know raised a laugh but made a valid point when he reported his experience of formally trying to teach his child the letter/sound correspondences in books she enjoyed listening to. 'She behaved as if she thought I was mad! It was fun for all of five minutes. I've never succeeded in getting her back to it, but she does enjoy stories.' I know this feeling myself. I once asked a small girl, rather stupidly, 'What does that letter say?' She cupped her ear to the page and then, hearing nothing, looked up at me and shrugged. If you have put in place the building blocks by introducing your child to the pleasures and habits of looking at books, then when the time comes they will move into formal reading learning more easily because there will be no jarring, no change of pace from the time when as a baby they showed a determined effort to turn the page. Their learning will simply accelerate when confronted with the complicated symbols of print.

And just look what stories can teach! Simply telling children to be loving and compassionate, forgiving and non-violent, unselfish and honest is unlikely to work; but read them *Mr Gumpy's Outing* and Mr Gumpy's sheer unjustified kindness in the face of his friends' foolishness will seep into their thinking because the learning comes along with laughter, rhythm and action. In Shirley Hughes' *Dogger*, Dave's love for his rather moth-eaten toy dog Dogger, his sadness at Dogger's loss, his family's support and concern, his sister Bella's casual but monumental sacrifice for Dogger's retrieval – these things will take root. But none of them will happen unless we as parents make them. Reading skills, which need to be implanted by techniques, can only work if a strong interest is engendered first in the business of reading, and this is what parents are best at. 'Motivation' as it is often called is an absolutely essential condition for being a good reader. You might call it 'the tyrannosaurus syndrome' after those children who are so motivated by the study of dinosaurs that they can read the long, difficult and complex words used to name dinosaurs, words of the sort that they would never attempt in another context.

Family literacy professionals often point out that parents are their children's first and foremost teachers. Indeed research study after research study confirms what might seem obvious, that children whose families encourage literacy activities at home have higher reading achievement in early years at school and advanced language development. The presence of parents who spend time with their children; who read to them, who answer their questions and their requests for help; and who demonstrate in their own lives that reading is a rich source of relaxation, information and contentment is an essential pre-requisite for a child becoming a good reader at school. In particular being able to listen intently to stories is an important first step in learning to read. The child who is listening expertly is employing the senses and techniques which the mature reader uses; they are well on the road to reading. They are able to accept and mentally process a stream of written language and order ideas being presented, selecting the dominant and ignoring the irrelevant for maximum understanding of the author's message. If we create a habit of good listening then we are creating an environment in which children will want to learn to read. A very famous reading researcher, Marie Clay, put it this way: 'What the brain says to the eye is more important in reading than what the eye says to the brain.'

So some guidelines:

- Keep it simple: many parents have limited time to devote to working with their children. Reading to your child and encouraging them to read is sometimes enough. And especially don't force your child to sit and read when they want to do something else. That will be counterproductive.

- Reading to children should not cease when children can read independently. There is continuing value in reading aloud, perhaps a chapter or two at bedtime or an article from a newspaper. Perhaps parents can read with their children alternating pages or paragraphs. Maybe encourage the child to read to a family pet, a toy or a grandparent. All these things are legitimate forms of independent reading at home that will support success in children's literacy development.

- Some families will have time and access to a public library but if not ask if you can use the school library in the same way – perusing the books and taking books home after school.

- Learn the 'five finger rule'. A child opens a page in a book at random and begins to read, raising a finger each time they encounter an unknown word. If five fingers are raised before a page is complete the book is probably too challenging. It is, of course, fine to reread a favourite book and to read books that are 'too easy'. Don't we all from time to time do the same? And don't ignore internet reading. Screen reading is something we all do and which will be a major part of your child's future life.

- Remember that print can be found in many places – newspapers, magazines, mail, notes, shopping lists, street and shop signs, and songs. Captioned television is particularly useful – the child simultaneously hears and sees the words on the screen. There are a number of internet reading programmes that offer this experience of course.

Finally what about teens? At this age reading can often help oil the wheels of the sometimes fraught relationship with parents. Adolescents can sustain their relationship with their parents through reading material, discussing newspaper articles or borrowing their parents' paperbacks, for example. In one American study a mother reported, 'All these years my daughter had been secretly reading my novels of true crime, horror, suspense and romance, without me realising.' One teenager explained that his grandmother supplied his reading material because 'she goes to car boot sales and she knows I like Stephen King, so she'll pick up a book for me in that genre'. In this study adolescents also frequently talked about receiving books as presents for birthdays or Christmas.

So don't ignore your child's reading when they move to secondary school. Your influence still operates.

Reading studies all say quite clearly that what happens in the home makes a difference for better or for worse, at all ages, and those results should be comforting for parents. You can make a difference. Encouraging home reading need not be time consuming or complex. Instead parents can talk about books, encourage reading, answer questions initiated by their child and model their own literate behaviours. In doing this they are keeping the seventh commandment: Remember literacy to keep it holy.

YOU SHALL COVET FOR YOUR CHILD PLAY OF ALL TYPES

I lived in The Netherlands for seven years until 2015 and often admired the way Dutch parents seemed calm and confident in their role. In all the time I was there I never saw a Dutch parent shout at a child in public, and certainly never saw any child smacked. I was not surprised then by a 2013 Unicef report which rated Dutch children the happiest in the world, ahead of their peers in childhood well-being in comparison to twenty-nine of the world's richest countries. The UK came sixteenth and the USA twenty-sixth, just above Lithuania, Latvia and Romania – the three poorest countries in the survey. Children in The Netherlands were in the top fifth in each of the categories assessed – material well-being; health and safety; education; behaviours and risk; and housing and environment. When it came to Dutch children rating their own happiness levels, more than ninety-five per cent considered themselves happy. This Unicef report was a follow-up to one conducted in 2007 when the UK and USA ranked in the two lowest positions and again The Netherlands was at the top of the league.

Commentators have suggested that the main reason for this high happiness rating is that Dutch children enjoy freedoms denied to children in other countries: Dutch children have little or no homework at primary school, they are trusted to ride their bikes to school on their own from as young as seven (along cycle paths that are completely separate from roads) and allowed to play outside unsupervised. They have regular family meals and spend significant amounts of time with their mothers and fathers as well as grandparents; they enjoy simple pleasures and are happy with second-hand toys. Indeed, there is a famous annual day in The Netherlands, King's Day in April, when children lay out their toys on blankets and sheets in streets and in markets around the country to swap and sell cheaply. It's the kind of childhood that many parents in other European countries are nostalgic for. Children start school at four but don't officially start structured learning – reading, writing, number work – until they are six years old. If they do show interest in this kind of learning early on then they are encouraged and allowed to explore for themselves and supported, but not pushed in any way. They are encouraged to be independent and often left to get on with things themselves. Dutch parents will not do for their children things the children might be able to do for themselves. In the Unicef study Dutch children are among the least likely to feel pressured by school work and scored highly in finding their classmates helpful and friendly. The Dutch don't seem concerned about their child being the cleverest. They seem to want them to be easy-going and happy. The Dutch have a realistic perspective on parenthood, and understand that their children are far from perfect. Of course, they still struggle with the realities and messiness of everyday life, but perhaps because they are more forgiving of their own shortfalls and those of their children they are able to enjoy parenthood.

It seems to me that these positive aspects of parenthood in The Netherlands are the results of a Dutch culture that is centred around home, family and play. Of course, often both parents go out to work but The Netherlands has the highest percentage of workers on part-time contracts. Most Dutch parents consider the chance to be at home with their children a privilege. Both parents also share equally the parenting tasks. It is far more common to see a father out on his own with his children than in the UK, and often too grandparents are around to support.

Crucially the Dutch place their children's well-being at the heart of what they do. Parents have a healthy attitude to children, seeing them as individuals rather than extensions of themselves. They understand that achievement doesn't necessarily lead to happiness, but that happiness can cultivate achievement. Dutch parenting style is, it seems, a happy balance between parental involvement and benign neglect. Play is more important than being quietly obedient in social situations. Children are asked to explore the world around them and learn from that. This means though that play can be noisy and disruptive in public spaces, something that would be frowned upon in the UK. In fact, I have been annoyed myself in Dutch restaurants where a group of children are allowed to run around the tables playing games, but other Dutch guests do not seem to notice.

This Dutch way of raising children who are happy is not complicated. Beneath the madness of modernity, the basics of raising a happy child haven't really changed. One final example from The Netherlands will make this point. According to the 2013 Unicef report, eighty-five per cent of Dutch children have breakfast every day, sitting down to eat at a table with the family before the school or working day starts. In no other country do families meet for breakfast so regularly. Of course, there is a great deal of research which suggests that a good breakfast is beneficial in all sorts of ways. It stops snacking on unhealthy food during the morning, it reduces obesity and it increases the ability to concentrate. But the major benefit is that the day starts with the family together around the breakfast table, a calming and bonding experience.

So what has all this got to do with the eighth commandment: You shall covet for your child play of all types? Well, it is about allowing children time to be children, to be free to play, just as you see all young mammals doing. The Dutch love the outdoors. The outside tables in cafés stay open all year round, people cycle in all weathers, and in the summer many head south for camping holidays. Children pick up on this attitude. They go out, to play outside and to visit their friends, in all weathers, which allows them a huge degree of freedom. Sporting activities are rarely cancelled as a result of bad weather. Playing outside in all weathers is a rite of passage, and if children get wet with muddy clothes and messed up hair, then that is hardly commented upon. Independent outdoor play is seen as an antidote to raising passive, media-addicted, lazy children.

Early childhood experts have been explaining for decades that play provides children with enjoyable experiences and opportunities to develop physical and social skills, and contributes to intellectual development, not to mention promoting habits of perseverance – 'stick-to-it-ness' – and flexible behaviour. Parents who want to be good enough need not only to encourage play and provide sufficient opportunities, but also to show respect by actually becoming involved in play activities. Play is such an important skill. It is said that we grow old because we stop playing. We don't stop playing because we grow old. You might ask yourself, for instance, when was the last time you had fun at work? Of course, take your work seriously, but it is a grave error to take yourself too seriously. I was caught out doing this myself once in a playground. A young child handed me a plastic teacup half-filled with a thick and murky mixture. Thinking I was joining in the game, I sat down and pretended to drink. 'Thank you so much. This is delicious tea,' I said. 'Don't be silly, Martin,' said the child, 'it's just mud and water.'

There are American education adverts that say college begins in the kindergarten. No it doesn't. Your first steps in schooling begin in the kindergarten, not your university career. A three year old isn't half a six year old, she's a three year old. And a ten year old isn't a half-formed twenty year old. Childhood is not some kind of waiting room for adulthood. It's a period of growth and merit in itself in which play has a crucial role. Playing is integral to children's enjoyment of their lives, their health and their development. Children and young people whatever their age, culture, ethnicity or social and economic background, need and want to play, indoors and out, in whatever way they can. Through playing, children are developing their abilities, exploring their creativity and learning about themselves, other people and the world around them.

Play England (www.playengland.org.uk) is a body that promotes play and has set out a statement of the value of play in its charter. It says that play is the fundamental way that children enjoy their childhood. It is essential to their quality of life as children:

- Playing is fun: it is how children enjoy themselves.

- Play promotes children's development, learning, imagination, creativity and independence.

- Play can help to keep children healthy and active.

- Play allows children to experience and encounter boundaries, learning to assess and manage risk in their lives, both physical and social.

- Play helps children to understand the people and places in their lives, learn about their environment and develop their sense of community.

- Play allows children to find out about themselves, their abilities, their interests and the contribution they can make.

- Play can be therapeutic. It helps children to deal with difficult or painful circumstances, such as emotional stress or medical treatment.

- Play can be a way of building and maintaining important relationships with friends, carers and family members.

If you were to ask people who are over forty years old what their favourite place was as a child, I guess the majority will recall some outdoor place – a street where they played football, a den in a nearby park, a children's playground. Ask children of today the same question and you would get a completely different answer. My generation spent their childhoods climbing trees and having adventures. I spent hours as a boy at a small local river, the Brent, catching leeches and keeping them in bottles for a time before releasing them back into the river – no doubt to be caught again on another day. Today's generation of children are mostly kept inside. These days, children are taught that the world is a scary place – be afraid, stay at home, don't take risks. But taking risks and meeting challenges are developmental imperatives for childhood. They give us confidence and courage. They help in later life to face down fear and to work to fulfil our dreams. But if a parent displays anxiety then a child will easily pick up that message. Help your child to face their fears. Let them know you are there for them but do not rescue them. Can they balance on that wall? Of course they can if you hold their hand and help them jump off. The more you do the less space you leave them in which to learn. The more you take them away from something that won't really harm them, the more you collude with their belief that they cannot manage. Don't hold their bus or train ticket for them. Let them look after it themselves.

Children need and want to stretch and challenge themselves when they play, so allowing your child exciting play allows them to encounter and learn about risk, build confidence, learn skills and develop resilience. Children are primed for risk taking – studies show that their brains do not register danger in the same way that adult brains do. So your duty to keep your child safe is bound to come into conflict with your duty to give them freedom to explore and develop. You can, of course, warn them of dangers – for teenagers of smoking, drugs and alcohol, for instance, even though teenagers are unlikely to listen to a lecture on these topics – parents in their view are inevitably misinformed! The best approach is to be calm and rational and approach potential problems from the perspective of 100 per cent trust. The odd thing is that when people expect to be trusted, most often they live up to that expectation. This sometimes means being able to tolerate one's own anxiety. My youngest daughter was something of a daredevil and loved jumping off high boards at swimming pools after she had learned to swim at seven years old – diving boards much higher above the water than I have ever been able to cope with. I sat watching with trepidation as she disappeared under the water having jumped, and then in fear for a few anxious seconds until she appeared on the surface again. Of course, there have to be boundaries to risk, especially physical. You would not send a child who has just learned to ski down a piste on their own, or a child who has just been given a new bike out on to a busy road without helmet and a chaperone. On the other hand, being an overprotective parent can also do damage.

There is a movement in the US called 'free-range parenting'. It was started accidently by a journalist, Lenore Skenazy, in 2008, when she had the wild idea to let her nine-year-old son ride the New York subway on his own. He lived! But Skenazy was immediately branded 'America's worst mum' in the press, and so she launched a blog: freerangekids. com. The presumption of this movement is that children are in more danger from being kept in home 'batteries' and fed on TV and games, than they are in being allowed to roam free in their nearby fields. They point out that our society is actually safer than it has ever been (child abductions, though terrible when they happen, are incredibly rare) and violent crime is declining (in the US by fifteen per cent in the past decade according to the FBI). On the other hand, the number of children suffering from anxiety, eating disorders and nervous afflictions of various sorts is skyrocketing. So if you want to avoid your child being anxious it might be best to stop watching their every movement. Good parenting teaches children many things but among them is not to be afraid of doing new things, to take evaluated risks, to live life adventurously and perhaps the satisfaction of completing something that was not altogether pleasant at the time. We should allow children to take calculated risks, and then learn from mistakes. Don't you think it is always better to try things, to live adventurously, rather than lead a life where you constantly wonder 'if only I had'?

Finally, go easy on buying commercial toys. Most parents know that young children can get as much fun out of a large cardboard box as they can from an expensive plastic game. My eldest daughter who studied anthropology at university taught me about 'gift communities'. A transactional relationship is where you pay X for Y, but 'gift' relationships are where a person borrows sugar from a neighbour, or where someone intends to buy some nails and you say: 'I've got some, I'll give you mine.' This works because of the lack of exactitude. It makes those involved feel that they are beholden to the other because they are not quite sure of the equality of the gift. This creates interesting cultural glue. There are whole societies in what is usually called the developing world still based on this principle. It makes sense if you think about it. Some aspects of our consumerism are daft. Now we go down a street and there are forty little lawns and everybody owns a lawn mower. They use it only once a week at most.

With an average child's Christmas gifts adding up to hundreds of pounds is it any wonder that our children are tempted by consumerism? Two generations ago, in fact when I was a child, most children would have had a handful of treasured toys and looked after them for years. The pedal car and the train set my granny gave me still hold strong, happy memories, but they were my one Christmas gift. The sack I left at the end of my bed for Santa was always full, but mostly filled by my parents with trinkets and bulked up with an apple and an orange, and if I was lucky, a box of sweets. Now the Unicef global report on child well-being found that British parents are trapping their children in a cycle of 'compulsive consumerism', which is not a recipe for making children happier. Having more possessions as a child is no more likely to make you happy then being very rich as an adult will. Instead research has found that children will be more satisfied with their lives if we train them to appreciate what they already have – to teach them gratitude. In one experiment with eleven to thirteen year olds, researchers at New York's Hofstra University asked two groups of pupils to keep a diary for two weeks. One set was asked to write five things they were grateful for each day. The other was asked to write five things that annoyed them. Afterwards the students who noted the good things reported feeling happier with their lives than their peers, and this technique is now seen as a useful everyday tool to get children to focus on what they do have, rather than what they don't. Appreciating what you have in life is the way to happiness; being dissatisfied or envious is not.

All this adds up to a simple message: you should let your children play, and give them time to play, but it is not necessary to buy them lots of things to play with. You can support your child's play by respecting the value and importance of all types of play, playing with him or her, and by creating opportunities and allowing time for children to play independently with their friends, inside and outside the home. Become a bit Dutch! Covet for your child play of all types.

YOU SHALL COVET GOOD RELATIONS WITH YOUR PARTNER AND FAMILY MEMBERS

The combined efforts of two parents are additive, i.e. one and one really does add up to more than two! There are two obvious things that help if you want to have happy children: remain married and stay alive. I have failed miserably in one of those areas but am, happily, still succeeding in the other. In fact, research suggests that one in four children in the UK can expect their parents to be living separately by the age of sixteen. It is important then to consider your relationship with your husband/wife/partner and in discussing how to have happy children.

Unfortunately for many men, after children arrive they come to the painful revelation that the woman they adore now gets all her intimacy needs met by being a mother. There is no longer an arm around the shoulder, a fleeting touching of hands, a gentle hug. Humanising contact is between the parent and the child and not between the parents. This can lead to the gradual disintegration of the bond between adult partners. For instance, it might seem to make sense for the mother to sleep in another room because she is breastfeeding and getting up in the night disturbs her partner, but the signal might be a less pragmatic one. Similarly if parents never go out together without the children, is it a signal that they are so preoccupied with the children and their children's activities and emotional states that the intimacy in the parents' relationship is getting lost? The paradox is this: to focus fully and only on your children will come with a cost to the relationship with your partner that many children will depend on for stability and security. Thinking only about the children unbalances the healthy equilibrium between giving attention to partners, to work and to children. If the Western world seems now more child-centric, then it is perhaps no coincidence that the divorce rate is also steep – forty-two per cent in England and Wales according to the latest Office for National Statistics figures. It is very difficult to spend your time rolling out the red carpet for your children, where everything has to be planned and researched to give the best experience for your child – where the project to raise a child is all-consuming – and still have a committed, connected relationship. We all have only so much energy.

A marital therapist, Andrew G. Marshall, has written a book on how to child-proof your marriage. It is called *I Love You But You Always Put Me Last*. In that book he asks the reader how long they would stay with someone who was telling them on a daily basis that they were of no significance. He reports that his clients get very upset with him when he tells them that marriage is for a lifetime but children are just passing through. Of course, the world is never as simple as this, and black and white language, which suggests it's the children or the marriage, is not particularly helpful. Bringing up children makes demands on your time and it is an effort to remember to pay attention to the other significant person in your life, but if you don't pay attention to your partner's needs you are unlikely to be doing your best for the children. A 2015 study by Relate, the marriage guidance organisation, found that couples with children were far more likely to have had no sex in the past month (forty-three per cent) than those without kids (twenty-six per cent). And sixty-one per cent of parents cite money worries as a primary relationship stress as compared with forty-seven per cent of couples without children. These figures highlight the pressures of raising children, running a household and working, all of which may put a strain on partner relationships. Nevertheless, although it is a strain, it is the case that what's best for children is to see parents loving each other. Children are resilient, they can be fitted into family life, rather than family life fitted around them. Small things matter. It only takes thirty seconds to give someone a hug or kiss; those thirty seconds as a couple will mean a lot. Linger over hellos and goodbyes. It will start to make a difference. Relate to each other first and together to the children, and not to each other through the children. And it will be helpful to your child also if on occasions you sit down with your partner and think about the division of parenting responsibilities. Do both parents monitor after-school activities, attend parent-teacher conferences and help with homework? If both parents read with their children and both attend school functions, if they take it in turns to prepare breakfast for example, then the emotional climate within which children are raised is more likely to be a positive one.

It would be wrong to imagine, however, that if there are no stresses in a marriage then everything is fine or vice versa. If there is no disagreement there is no challenge to each other, and no personal growth. There is something wrong if parents don't disagree with each other from time to time. Most people have heard of those marriages that last seven years and then fall apart, and the couple says: 'I don't know what happened. We never argued.' That perhaps was the problem. Perhaps these people were not really in a marriage at all. If problems and issues never get to the surface, one person never knows what the other was really thinking. If each partner is too nervous to say something contradictory to the other, this suggests there is something fundamentally wrong with the relationship. Serious conflict is bad but disagreement and challenge is not. And children intuitively understand this. Of course, it is not great for children to listen to parents have a stand-up row, but they can usually quite confidently cope with parents who argue at low temperatures. Alleviate some of the fears by talking with them and sharing some simple facts. Even though some couples who argue end up getting divorced it doesn't mean that every time mum and dad argue they are thinking of separating.

However, if a marriage does fall apart, it is not all bad news for the children. Although there is considerable debate regarding the effects of divorce or the death of a parent on children, most scholars agree that divorce and parental death do have an important influence on the life course of children. Past research has consistently found that children of divorced parents are at greater risk of mental health problems and experience lower educational attainment, though of course neither of these things are inevitable – they are simply statistically more likely. However, researchers have become much more circumspect about the negative consequences of parental divorce in recent years. The assumption that parental divorce is necessarily harmful to the emotional well-being of children has been challenged by longitudinal research (e.g. Strochschein 2005). In other words, by comparing children whose parents later divorce and those whose parents remain married, researchers have discovered that many of the childhood problems that were thought to be the result of divorce were in fact often in existence prior to the divorce. So although the potential negative effects of divorce or the death of a parent on the well-being of children is well documented, the effect doesn't inevitably have to be bad. I once overheard my youngest (possibly in justification of her situation) saying to a friend: 'I quite like my parents living separately. I get two lots of holidays and two lots of Christmas presents!'

In any case there are things you can do to reduce the negative effects of parents splitting up. How do you stop your children getting hurt? The children's mental health charity Place2Be says the key message for divorcing parents is that they have to put more effort into the love they have for their children than into the animosity that they may have for each other. Where possible arrangements for the children should be drawn up immediately. An informal written agreement set up straight away can often bypass future arguments about sharing the children. Children obviously can be harmed by the fall-out from unpleasant legal battles about residency and 'contact arrangements'. Making a big song and dance about contact is not helpful to the children. Sometimes it becomes a point of pride that your children stay with you for a night or more, when all the evidence suggests that children do not care as much as parents about 'staying over'. They do care about seeing both parents but what they care about most is there being no more arguments. On the other hand, be careful about rushing into post-divorce family outings. Going out as a family when you have broken up is not necessarily the best thing for children. It can be confusing and give them false hope. What is more important is working towards being able to stand together on the side of the school football pitch or together attend a school parents' evening without obvious tension or worse hurling abuse at each other. Above all, make sure that your kids understand that when two people divorce they aren't divorcing their children. Let your children know that when divorce happens both their parents will still love them and will continue to care for them.

Children benefit from clear communication about their new and changing living arrangements. Children want to know what is happening. Most children want to be told the truth. They are usually able to see straight through secrets and evasions. Keeping relevant information from the children can actually increase their feelings of distress and despair. Parents can be seen to be united as one team, even if they are no longer married to each other. It is not a given that you turn into good cop/bad cop. Parental agreements, i.e. the extent to which parents agree on topics, such as behavioural expectations and moral values, is an indicator of the level of consistency which children receive from both parents, which they need for clarity and not confusion. Disagreements about child-rearing issues have been linked to child behaviour problems in children and psychological distress in adolescence. Conversely, equally supportive parenting from both mother and father have been significantly associated with cognitive competence and well-being. But getting parental practices lined up between you is not very helpful if at the same time the emotional atmosphere is stressful for the child. That atmosphere is largely to do with demandingness and responsiveness. One reason why divorce is problematic for children is that parental preoccupations with their own problems during divorce may interfere with normal parenting. This is not always neglect. A mother may for instance employ more warmth to a 'smothering' level as a compensating mechanism if her partner has left her feeling lonely. Is there a reason you need your child to love you more than your partner or former partner? A father may withdraw from a close relationship with his child as emotional protection against the hurt of being without them. Are your feelings more important than your child's?

Parents are not the only significant adults in a child's life. If they are at school then teachers may well play an important role, but even more significant are grandparents. Grandparents are really important backstage figures, who sometimes come front stage. When I was still a baby my parents entered a training college in London, which didn't allow children to board with them – a rule quite difficult to understand now. I was packed off to my grandmother who lived in Leigh-on-Sea in Essex, and I spent a good part of the first two years of my life with her. I loved being with her throughout my childhood and still have very vivid and fond memories of sitting drinking lemon cordial in the sun on her garden swing, and feeding apples to the milkman's horse that used to visit her front gate. We used to make marmalade together in a warm kitchen. And I remember being taught how to polish shoes by my grandfather. My grandmother bought me a sailing boat, which I took down to the saltwater pool at the edge of a muddy beach and sailed to my heart's content for hours. You will have, no doubt, similar fond memories of your grandparents. Later, whenever I was unhappy or fed up with my parents, I used to run away to my grandmother's house and once got caught by a guard at Fenchurch Street railway station in London and carted home before I could make it onto the train. Such is the influence of grandparents.

There can be no clear guidelines on how to be a grandparent – that will depend, of course, on individual family circumstances. But the dramatic rise in the last twenty years of the number of children in professional day care suggests that grandparents are not now being called upon to provide the extensive nurturing and caretaking functions that in the past was a common role. Grandparents themselves may be confused about how they can be part of their adult children's lives and grandchildren's lives without being intrusive. In fact, several researchers have suggested that the beneficial influence of grandparents is most likely if there is neither too little nor too much contact. The relationship between grandchildren and grandparents is unique in the sense that it is exempt from the emotional intensity and responsibility that exists in parent/child relationships. It has been said that the love, nurturance and acceptance which grandchildren find in the grandparents/grandchildren relationship confers a natural form of social immunity on children that they cannot get from any other person. Research on the role and effect of grandparenting is sparse but one in-depth study of the relationship between grandchildren and grandparents suggests that this emotional attachment is a fundamental component of a child's well-being. So, although under ordinary circumstances interaction with parents and peers dominates the social lives of children, especially during the early years, the importance of grandparents' indirect influence on children, even though they may not be directly present, is hard to underestimate. What then can be said about the involvement of grandparents in their grandchildren's lives?

Grandparents can have all sorts of roles in the life of a child: as the link between family members; as a constant in the life of a child – either through direct personal experience, or through stories if they are no longer alive; as teachers of basic skills; as negotiators between children and their parents, helping each to understand the other; as a model for adulthood; as a connector to the past giving a sense of historical rootedness to the child; as a determiner of how the young feel about the old; as 'great parents' providing a secure and loving adult/child relationship, which is next in emotional importance to parents. With attachment to grandparents comes the experience of being loved, accepted, a sense of security and warmth, a historical sense of self and the gift of a role model for one's future ageing, which will be opened much later in life.

Traditionally grandparents spoil their grandchildren, but this is not really the best way to establish good relations with grandchildren and as a parent you should be wary of this happening. Financial support from grandparents to parents is certainly an important factor in the quality of life of some children whose parents are not affluent, but no doubt you want your child to associate their grandparents with love, not with gifts. Better is to give the gift of 'being there'. When grandchildren and grandparents become involved in shared activities their relationship helps the children learn about themselves and their families. Many of the activities that grandparents can do with children assist children to develop skills that can easily transfer to and enhance school learning. So grandparents can provide a helpful adult resource and facilitate children's learning and they can also contribute to children's social development. Often grandparents supply the extra support that some children need to have a sense of self-worth and to feel nurtured. Grandparents are better for children if they see themselves as informal teachers rather than sources of treats and gifts. Grandchildren who learn with and from their grandparents will form strong bonds with them. The grandchildren will benefit from knowing that they are important enough for grandparents to spend time with them. And they will have a model to enhance their relationships with their own children in the future.

We know that children learn through play – see The Eighth Commandment – especially when they encounter activities that encourage them to explore, think and communicate. These are the types of activities that grandchildren and grandparents can share. Grandparents who talk, read and listen carefully to their grandchildren provide positive modelling. Favourite books can be read to and with children, the contents and illustrations discussed as they read. And grandparents might sometimes offer books which reflect their interests, explaining their particular hobbies to their grandchildren in the expectation that children will be very intrigued by what their grandparents like to do in their daily lives. Grandparents have interesting stories to tell about their life experiences and families. They may have photo albums that record family birthdays, weddings and holidays. When children observe and listen to talk about these things they are enhancing not just their emotional development but also their cognitive and language skills. When grandparents teach songs to their grandchildren the children learn about history and culture, create memories and strengthen social bonds. Children are not music critics and will not judge the musical quality of the songs!

Grandparents today have fewer grandchildren than in previous generations. However, they also have longer life expectancy and often an increased quality of life so they have more time and energy to spend with grandchildren. The best relationships between grandparents and grandchildren are companionable and these relationships are most easily established by grandparents who live near their grandchildren, and can provide company, play and affection. But it is not impossible to establish this kind of intimate relationship even if living some distance away – via email, Skype, social media and mutual visits – and sharing aspects of their daily lives. A family website that keeps grandchildren informed of the activities of the extended family network can lead to increased understanding of family connections and heritage. A video diary of the children's development and accomplishments can help interactions between grandchildren and grandparents. Grandparents who are geographically remote can still be emotionally linked to their grandchildren.

When a couple become parents they are immediately promoted into the 'middle generation' of a three-generation family. They become the bridge between the generations below and above them. In this sense parents hold a great deal of power in the process of building relations between their own mother and father and their children. So parents are crucial in the nature of the relationship between grandparents and grandchildren. It is as well to remember then that parental feelings towards grandparents are easily transmitted towards children and these feelings and attitudes will persist throughout children's lives. Parents model relations with older members of the family and often children will take their cue from how their parents relate to the grandparents. Many studies in the 1980s established that women are particularly important in this regard. They tend to be the ones who maintain the ties between family sub-systems. The implication of this is that children more often become involved with the maternal grandparents than their father's parents. Maternal grandmothers are visited more frequently and viewed as more emotionally close than are paternal grandparents. This is the usual pattern, so some diplomacy is involved in ensuring that the other set of grandparents do not feel 'left out'.

How divorce between parents affects children's relationships with their grandparents is open to debate – sometimes, of course, a parent withdraws their children from continuing relationships with their former partner's parents – and you can see from what is said above that this is a mistake – but often divorce can reinforce strong relations between grandparents and grandchildren, with grandparents functioning as surrogate parents and as mediators of anxiety and tension. In addition, of course, new partners come onto the scene and then children have to negotiate a relationship with their new 'grandparents'. Or children may be faced with learning to share grandparents with newly acquired siblings. All these complications should not distract from the fundamental truth: the grandchild/grandparent relationship is so important that parents would be wise to try to maintain it in whatever circumstances they find themselves.

Being part of a family gives a child the wonderful feeling they will be loved for the rest of their life, and it teaches them how to love, something much more important than wealth or privilege. It is not *what* we have that is important, but *who* we have. So heed the ninth commandment: You shall covet good relations with your partner and family members.

YOU SHALL TAKE FOR THYSELF POSITIVE THINKING

I once heard Benjamin Zander, conductor of the Boston Symphony Orchestra, talking about his father. His father had escaped from Germany at the beginning of World War II just before he would have been taken to the extermination camps. His sister was not so lucky and was placed in a cattle truck and never seen again. Benjamin's father arrived in England and was immediately interned as a German. He left England after the war with no money or possessions, but never complained about his life once and was never anything else but positive. And his final act was in the same manner. He was on his deathbed, and Benjamin Zander's brother, a doctor, knocked on the door one morning to see if his father was OK or needed anything. As he poked his head around the door a weak voice from the bed replied to him: 'I'm fine. Is there anything I can do for you, son?' In the same talk Benjamin Zander explained how he deals with problems. When he is teaching, or there is a problem with a rehearsal, he doesn't berate anybody or complain, but normally says 'How fascinating!' and throws his arms wide in a gesture of embrace of the problem. I suggest that's a good way to approach many problems. Think: 'how fascinating!' It might be a bit difficult on the golf course when you've hit a duff shot or in a slow airport queue when you are late for your flight, but try it anyway. Did you know optimists live seven years longer than pessimists on average? Moaning kills you! So try to make sure you don't condone your children complaining. Tell them the story of the man returning home from work in the family car. When his wife asked how his day had been he said: 'The good news is that the airbag worked.'

The 'power of positive thinking' is a popular concept, and the original book by Norman Vincent Peale with that name has spawned an industry. Sometimes the idea can feel a little cliché, but the physical and mental benefits of positive thinking have been demonstrated by multiple scientific studies. In particular, positive thinking can give you more confidence and improve your mood. It is just as dispiriting to hear children complain as it is adults. To be sure there is enough, even in the rich Western world, to complain about: too much bureaucracy and administrative paperwork, computer crashes, a new piece of work popping up late on Friday afternoon, the stresses of travel. Children will have their own potential complaints: they didn't get the plate of food they wanted, they have too much homework, their favourite toy is broken. Such complaints are common and normal. More important is if they complain about life more generally and think perhaps that they are a failure. The fundamental needs of children are to be happy and emotionally resilient, excited to learn and feeling loved for who they are, knowing that they can face challenges and not fear failure. Success will not follow your child everywhere, but children are usually optimistic, so if your child starts to adopt a negative attitude and fears failure then it is worth taking note. It is helpful to point out that success often consists of going from failure to failure without loss of enthusiasm; rather than thinking you have failed, to simply thinking you have delayed success. James Dyson, who made his fortune from domestic electrical goods, has reported that he made 5126 prototypes of the various parts of his famous vacuum cleaner before he finally got it right. There were 5126 failures, but he learned from each one, so it didn't matter. Fear of failure and negative thinking can be crippling. It is important for children to learn that trying things and not being successful will teach you how to push yourself. Telling your children 'You can do anything' isn't as effective as showing them they can overcome failure by encouraging them to 'stick at it'. Failing at something can be simply a step on the road to success, and there is no greater success than working hard, trying new things and overcoming your weaknesses.

One good way to promote positive thinking in your child is simply to talk to them honestly about their attitude to life. I say 'simply', but this is easier said than done. When is it best to talk intimately to your children, to discuss serious things? The simplest answer is when they decide to talk to you. It is only too common to ask a child about her day and get nothing in return – actually more likely with a 'him' – but then, when you least expect it, a child can release a fascinating insight into their social or emotional world. Often those golden moments happen when you are doing something else. Children can have an uncanny knack of seeking your attention just when it is most inconvenient, but if you recognise when those moments are you can enjoy great conversation with your children. So pick your time. For instance, a teenager's body clock works differently. Before 10 a.m. it will be hard to get anything more than a word or two at best out of them, but after 10 p.m. they can be positively talkative. If you can catch them within an hour of their bedtime you'll be surprised how much they will reveal. Of course, conversation is a two-way street, so when are you in the best form for talking to them? Is it when everyone is rushing around in the morning trying to get ready for school and work, hungry and ready for breakfast? At this time of day you are probably just happy they have managed to put their clothes on correctly. Obviously you have to talk logistics and business at this time of day, but it's not a great time to offer advice or probe some area of their life you want to know about. Similarly if you come home from work stressed out and tired, best give yourself some time to wind down and relax before you attempt too much intimate conversation. Wait and take advantage of your elevating mood as the evening progresses.

So what do you say in these conversations about being positive? Discuss, for instance, how a morning mood can set the tone for the rest of the day. So suggest that they start the day with positive affirmations. Talk to yourself in the mirror even if you feel silly, with statements like 'Today will be a good day.' Talk about focusing on the good things, however small. Almost invariably, you're going to encounter obstacles throughout the day – there's no such thing as a perfect day. For example, if the school canteen has run out of your favourite food, think about the thrill of trying something new. Talk about being able to laugh about it when things go wrong. How fascinating! You mess up a painting you wanted to bring home from class to show Grandma. No problem, look at the wonderful, colourful mess! Talk about turning negative thoughts into positive. You might think 'I'm so bad at this' or 'I shouldn't have tried that', but these thoughts turn into feelings and might cement your view of yourself. When you catch yourself doing this, stop and replace those thoughts with positive ones. For example, 'I'm so bad at this' becomes 'Once I get more practice, I'll be much better at this'. 'I shouldn't have tried' becomes 'That didn't work out as planned – maybe next time'. Talk about finding positive friends. When you surround yourself with positive people, you'll hear positive outlooks, positive stories and positive affirmations. Their positive words will sink in and affect your own line of thinking.

The test of whether you have managed to bring up happy children will be the measure of their independence. I asked my eldest daughter once, when she was in her late teens, what the test of my parenting might be. She was a bit flummoxed. So I suggested, 'How about the test is whether you can stop denting my bank account?' And then, knowing that she despised social media personalities I said, rather cruelly I have to admit, 'Look at Paris Hilton or Kim Kardashian. They're not denting their parents' bank account are they?' If your child is still inhabiting your spare room – that's not a great advert for successful parenting surely? A positive, independent spirit should be one of your ambitions for your child. I mean not just financial independence, of course, but independence of thought, social independence and good mental health. Your job in bringing up happy children is, in the end, to make yourself redundant. So heed the tenth commandment: You shall take for thyself positive thinking. You should want your children, when they leave school, to throw off the bowlines, sail away from your safe harbour and catch the trade winds in their sails. You should want them to explore, dream and discover.

REFERENCES

1. YOU SHALL NOT BE PERFECT

Bettelheim, B, *A Good Enough Parent*, Knopf, 1987.

2. YOU SHALL PREFER PRESENCE TO PRAISE

Baddaley, L, *A Good Childhood: Valuing Children in Today's Society*, London, The Children's Society, 2014

Dweck, C, *Mindset: How You Can Fulfil Your Potential*, Ballantine Books, 2012.

Dweck, C, and Mueller, C, 'Praise for Intelligence Can Undermine Children's Motivation and Performance', *Journal of Personality and Social Psychology* , 1998, Vol 75 no 1, pp33–52.

Enright, A, *Making Babies: Stumbling into Motherhood* , Vintage, 2005.

Fulkerson, J, et al. '*Family Dinner Meal Frequency and Adolescent Development: Relationships with Developmental Assets and High-Risk Behaviours*', Journal of Adolescent Health , SAHM, 2006.

Grosz, S, *The Examined Life* , Chatto and Windus, 2013

Wilkie, M, and Nomaguchi, K, 'Does the Amount of Time Mothers Spend with Children and Adolescents Matter', *Journal of Marriage and Family*, Wiley, 2015.

3. YOU SHALL RESPECT CHANGE

Alix Spiegel National Public Radio broadcast on 11 September 2004, *Analysis: Studies on Psychology During Disasters*, 2004.

Dwyer, J and Flynn, K, *102 Minutes: The Untold Story of the Fight to Survive Inside the Twin Towers*, Arrow, 2005.

4. YOU SHALL NOT MAKE FOR YOURSELF A FALSE IDOL IN SCREEN TIME, BUT COVET SLEEP TIME

British Broadcasting Corporation, *BBC's response to the Department of Culture, Media and Sport's Green Paper: Audience appendix*, 2016.

Carey, T, *Mum Hacks*, Crimson, 2016.

Giaquinta, J, Bauer, J, and Levin, J, *Beyond Technology's Promise: An Examination of Children's Educational Computing at Home*, Cambridge University Press, 1993.

Janis-Norton, N, *Calmer, Easier, Happier, Screen Time*, Hodder and Stoughton, 2016.

Jiang, X, Hardy, L and Baur, L, et al. *Sleep Duration Schedule and Quality Among Urban Chinese Children*, PlosOnebit.ly/sleepduration, 2015.

The Office of Communications, *Communications Market Report*, UK, 2017.

Public Health Ontario, *Children Not Getting Enough Sleep? How Parents Providing Support Can Make All the Difference*, BMC Public Health, 2017.

Sax, L, *The Collapse of Parenting: How We Hurt Our Children When We Treat Them Like Grown-Ups*, Basic Books, 2015.

Woodard, E, Alexander, A and Lemish, D, *Media In the Home; The Fifth Annual Survey of Parents and Children*, Annenberg Public Policy Center, Philadelphia, 2000.

5Rights Foundation, *Digital Childhood*, 2018.

5. YOU SHALL TAKE CARE OF YOUR CHILD'S FRIENDSHIPS

Freud, A, *The Ego and the Mechanisms of Defence*, English translation, 1937, Hogarth Press, 1936.

Newcomb, A and Bagwell, C, *Children's Friendship Relations, a Meta-Analysis*, Cambridge University Press, 1995.

NSW Kids and Families, *Why Children Matter*, New South Wales Government, Australia, 2016.

Rubin, K, Bukowski, W, and Laursen, B, *Handbook of Peer Interactions, Relationships and Groups*, Guildford Press, 2011.

The Children's Society, *The Good Childhood Report*, annual survey produced in conjunction with The University of York, 2017.

6. YOU SHALL HONOUR DISCIPLINE

Reddy, A, *The Art of Mindfulness for Children: Mindfulness Exercises That Will Raise Happier, Confident, Compassionate, and Calmer Children*, Createspace Independent Publishing, 2014.

Snel, E, *Sitting Still Like a Frog: Mindfulness Exercises for Kids (and Their Parents)*, Shambala Press, 2013.

7. REMEMBER LITERACY TO KEEP IT HOLY

Allington, R, et al. *Addressing Summer Reading Setback Among Economically Disadvantaged Elementary Students*, published online, Taylor and Francis, 2010.

Burningham, J, *Mr Gumpy's Outing*, Jonathan Cape, 2001.

Chandler, K, 'Reading Relationships: Parents, Adults and Popular Fiction', *Journal of Adolescent and Adult Literacy*, 43:3, 1999.

Clark, C, and Akerman, R, *Social Inclusion and Reading: An Exploration*, The National Literacy Trust, 2006.

Clark, C, and Foster, A, *Children and Young People's Reading Habits and Preferences*, The National Literacy Trust, 2005.

Clay, M, *Reading: The Patterning of Complex Behaviour*, Heinemann, 1979.

Hughes, S, *Dogger*, Mulberry, 1993.

Moyle, D, *Teaching Reading*, National Book League, 1977.

OECD, *Programme for International Student Assessment 2009 At A Glance*, Organisation for Economic Cooperation and Development, 2011.

8.   YOU SHALL COVET FOR YOUR CHILD PLAY OF ALL TYPES

Play England, *Charter for Children's Play*, published online 23 January 2009.

Strochschein, L, *Parental Divorce and Child Mental Health*, Wiley, 2005.

Unicef, *Child Well-being in Rich Countries*, Unicef Office of Research, 2013.

9.   YOU SHALL COVET GOOD RELATIONS WITH YOUR PARTNER AND FAMILY MEMBERS

Barranti, R, *The Grandparents/Grandchildren Relationship: Family Resource in an Era of Voluntary Bonds*, Family Relations, Vol 34, 3, 1985.

Chambers, J, Power, K, Loucke, N, and Swanson, V, 'The Interaction of Perceived Maternal and Paternal Parenting', *Journal of Adolescence*, Vol 24, 2, 2001.

Kornhaber, A, and Woodward, K, *Grandparents-Grandchildren: The Vital Connection*, Anchor Press/DoubleDay, 1981.

Link, M, Brubaker, E, and Brubaker, T, *Hand in Hand: Grandchildren and Grandparents Learning Together*, Educational Horizons, 2002.

Marshall, A G, *I Love You But You Always Put Me Last*, Pan MacMillan, 2015.

Meteyer, K, and Perry-Jenkins, M, *Dyadic Parenting and Children's Externalising Symptoms*, Family Relations 58 (289–302), 2009.

Relate, *The Way We Are Now: The State of the UK's Relationships*, relate.org.uk, 2016

10. YOU SHALL TAKE FOR THYSELF POSITIVE THINKING

Peale, N V, *The Power of Positive Thinking*, Ballantine Books, reissue edition, 1996.

ABOUT THE AUTHOR

Martin Coles has spent a lifetime working with and for children. His career includes being Primary School Headteacher in Oxfordshire, a Reader in Education at The University of Nottingham, The Head of Schools and Learning for Swindon Local Authority and the Principal of The British School in The Netherlands. Martin holds degrees from the universities of Oxford, London and Nottingham. He has two daughters and three grandchildren.

Find out more about
RedDoor Publishing and
sign up to our newsletter
to hear about our **latest
releases, author events,**
exciting **competitions**
and more at

reddoorpublishing.com

YOU CAN ALSO FOLLOW US:

 @RedDoorBooks

 RedDoorPublishing

 @RedDoorBooks